FACEBOOK
FANATIC

FACEBOOK FANATIC

EXPLODE YOUR POPULARITY, BUZZ YOUR BAND AND SECURE YOUR PRIVACY ON FACEBOOK

Editors of BottleTree Books LLC

BottleTree Books LLC

BottleTreeBooks.com

The 'Net You Need to Know™

FACEBOOK FANATIC

EXPLODE YOUR POPULARITY, BUZZ YOUR BAND AND SECURE YOUR PRIVACY ON FACEBOOK

First Edition
Manufactured in the United States and/or the United Kingdom
10 9 8 7 6 5 4 3 2 1
ISBN: 978-1-933747-06-4

Printed on recycled paper in both the United States and United Kingdom.

Contents

What You'll Experience

Jumpstart to Meeting People

Huge Popularity of Facebook

Facebook Networks   **Sign-Up**

Introduction
I

A. The Fascination with Facebook

Facebook.com began as a social networking site for Harvard college students to share information across the Web. Mark Zuckerberg started it and the concept took off in 2004. "Thefacebooks.com" later morphed into Facebook.com and the social networking site we have today. The idea spread across colleges all over the world and grew to include various high schools and corporate organizations.

Now anyone can join Facebook. By imposing few rules on its users, and allowing for free page creation, Facebook quickly became one of the most widely used sites on the Internet. It has over 30 million registered users and Facebook says it is adding around tens of thousands of new users a day. With this huge install base

The Facebook logo font appears to be Vecta Bold.

you will have hundreds if not thousands of other Facebook users that want to send you a message, post a comment on your Wall, browse through your photo albums, compare class schedules, and who are dying to be listed as *your* friend. No matter what your hobby or background, Facebook will open up a whole new world of people with the same interests.

In *Facebook Fanatic* you will learn how to make a killer Facebook profile with tips for adding the coolest photos, customizing your friend list, creating events, Noteing, The Wall, Facebook Development Platform, News Feeds, and how to Poke your friends. Key privacy settings are discussed at every level. You'll even learn how to get Facebook on your cell phone. With *Facebook Fanatic* you can create one of the most popular Facebook pages on the planet! So let's get started.

B. Facebook Connects You Instantly

If you have yet to sign-up at Facebook.com, you might wonder how its 30 million users are going to find *your* profile. After all, doesn't everyone on Facebook already have their own friends? Yes, people already on Facebook have a circle of online friends but most are looking to add new ones all the time. Chances are your real friends invited you to join Facebook in the first place so you can link them as Friends immediately via their email addresses.

> If you are a PC user, Internet Explorer and Firefox work best with Facebook. For Mac users, Safari and Firefox are the best browsers.

C. Facebook Networks Around the World

Facebook currently has one site at www.Facebook.com that provides access for its users worldwide. Think of Facebook as being organized into four main social networking areas: (1) Schools (High Schools & Colleges); (2) Companies; (3) Regions or Locations; and (4) None of the above. These are the Facebook networks. They can be found within the United States, Great Britain, Canada, Japan, Australia, Mexico, and several other countries, as well as many regions within them. If you want to suggest a new network, just click on Suggestions in the lower right-hand corner of any page and tell Facebook about it or follow this handy direct link: facebook.com/help.php?tab=suggest.

1. Schools on Facebook

Regarding schools, Facebook is growing in an attempt to reach every college student in the world so that users can network with other alumni or students. Remember, the site does trace its roots to Harvard. Follow this link to check if your college is on Facebook: http://www.facebook.com/networks/networks.php?view=college. If not, tell Facebook about it. Facebook is connected to over 22,000 high schools thus far. Under the old Facebook, high school students had to be invited to join Facebook (via email) by somebody from their high school already registered with Facebook. Now anyone can join. Many high schools issue school email accounts/addresses via Facebook. Check if your high school is on Facebook: http://www.facebook.com/networks.php?view=hs.

HIGH SCHOOL, COLLEGE, OR WORKPLACE NOT LISTED?
Keep in mind that Facebook is not connected everywhere *yet*. If you have found that your high school, college, or workplace is not supported visit: http://www.facebook.com/help.php?tab=newnetwork and make a request.

2. Companies on Facebook
Debating whether you want to join Facebook, yet you really don't want to be affiliated with your old college or alumni? Well, Facebook just might have your workplace online. Currently Facebook supports over 15,000 companies. Take a look and see who else is Facebooking at work: http://www.facebook.com/networks.php?view=companies.

3. Regions on Facebook
When you sign up on Facebook you can specify where you live to learn about various events happening in your region of the world and to meet new people who live close to you. Regions are segmented into cities on Facebook and in some instances countries or provinces: http://www.facebook.com/networks/networks.php?view=geographies.

NON-ENGLISH LANGUAGES ARE OK
At present, Facebook has limited its specific sites to English-speaking countries. There is no prohibition against using non-English languages within Facebook such as on The Wall or Notes, but you must register in English.

D. Facebook Sign-Up
Best of all, the Facebook sign-up process is easy and free. You simply input your profile information, layout your Facebook profile, and you are ready to meet new people. Facebook requires that you are at least 13 years of age or older to sign up. It

does not, however, verify the ages of members. There is a form you must fill out to create your account during the sign-up process. First input your name and the type of network you wish to belong to such as school or work, etc.

MUST USE REAL NAME

At present, Facebook requires that you use your real name. You do not, however, have to include your full last name. The first letter of your last name will suffice and you can put your nickname between your first and last names.

In creating your account, you must also enter your personal email address. This is what Facebook uses to send you notification emails. Next input your birth date (a lot of people fib here) and a mandatory password.

FACEBOOK SMS NUMBER

Facebook's text message number is 32665 or short code FBOOK. Do not expect a response from Mark Zuckerberg with over 30 million users!

Last, you must verify you are who you say you are by inputting your cellphone number. Facebook will then send a unique text message code to your phone. The code usually arrives immediately. Input it and you are verified for good.

WHAT TO DO IF YOU CANNOT CREATE AN ACCOUNT

If for some reason you are having trouble creating an account on Facebook, send an email to: info@facebook.com and tell Facebook where you are in the process and the trouble you are having. Put "Cannot Create Account" in the Subject line.

Contact Facebook Customer Service
Table 1.A
➢ Visit the following link: http://www.facebook.com/help.php?tab=suggest
➢ Give Facebook your issue or suggestion in the comments section

60 Second Summary

Key Introduction Tips

- Must be 13 or older to sign up for Facebook
- The three networks within Facebook are Schools, Workplaces, and Regions
- If you cannot create an account, explain the error in an email to info@facebook.com
- You can use non-English languages within Facebook

What You'll Experience

Before You Sign Up

Facebook Terms of Service

Privacy, Privacy, Privacy

Email Address & Privacy

II   Privacy & Terms of Service

A. Before You Sign Up

You should know what you are getting into before signing up for Facebook. Privacy of personal information is of utmost importance. Facebook collects two kinds of personal information. The first is that which you voluntarily give it such as your name, email address, age, etc. The second type of information you do not voluntarily disclose, but it collects anyway such as your computer's IP address. Facebook keeps *most* of your personal information private and confidential. Divulge only the amount you want to the Facebook community. The My Privacy area is obviously key to securing your privacy settings on Facebook, but there are other areas that are just as important. In this chapter we'll show you how to lock down your privacy on Facebook in all areas.

B. Facebook Privacy Policy

Facebook has one of the clearest privacy policies on the Web. Make sure you read it before signing up. Visit http://facebook.com/policy.php to view the Privacy Policy in its entirety. Here are key provisions of the policy for which you should be aware.

Know that Facebook is one of only a few social networking sites that has become a Member of TRUSTe, a non-profit organization that verifies whether Websites adhere to their privacy policies. Failure to comply with a policy can result in the TRUSTe certification being revoked.

If you have questions or concerns about Facebook's Privacy Policy, email them at privacy@facebook.com. If you do not get a response or it is unsatisfactory, file a complaint with TRUSTe at http://www.truste.org/consumers/watchdog_complaint.php and TRUSTe will act as your mediator with Facebook on the issue.

C. General Privacy Settings

With privacy you must start with the basics and build your security from there. Facebook already has a number of default privacy settings, which you can increase or decrease at any time. We will discuss each.

1. Types of Personal Information

Of course, the whole reason you join Facebook is to *disclose* information about yourself to build an online community of like friends. It is important to divulge only the amount of information you need to create a Facebook experience that is optimized for you, and not one piece of information more. Below is a list of the various types of information Facebook collects, how they are disclosed, and to whom.

Type	Info	Info Disclosed	To Whom
Full Profile Info	Age, Birthdate, Education, Email, Gender, First & Last Names, Interests, Password, Photo, City, Country, Zip Code	Age, Birthdate, City, Country, Education, Email, First & Last Names, Gender, Interests, Photos, Zip Code	Friends & Non-Friends within Networks if Profile Not Restricted
Non-Personally Identifiable Info	IP Address, Aggregate User Data, Browser	IP Address, Aggregate User Data, Browser	Facebook Third Party Vendors

Limited Profile Info	First & Last Names, Network Names, Photo, Profile Data (Number of Wall Posts)	First & Last Names, Network Names, Photo	Anyone Searching Facebook, Third Party Search Engines
Third Party Sources	Instant Messaging, Internet Notes, Magazines, Newspapers, Users of Facebook	Potentially All	Facebook or Third Parties

MORE SAFETY TIPS

Visit WiredSafety.org, CommonSense.com, BlogSafety.org, and OnGuardOnline.gov to learn even more safety tips about being private on the Web.

Even friends who are not Members of Facebook may have personal information stored by Facebook. The best example of this is when you send an email invite to a friend, asking them to join Facebook. The personal email address of your friend may be stored on Facebook's servers. If your friend wants it removed, they must contact Facebook at info@facebook.com and request its deletion.

2. Your Name

Facebook requires you to input your first name and at least the first letter of your last name when you sign up. Your first and last names are *always* shown on your profile. For privacy purposes, it is a good idea for almost anyone to use only the first letter of their last name on Facebook.

> If you are under the age of 21 (i.e., a minor in many countries), use only the first letter of your last name.

Let's say you get married and need to change your name on Facebook or simply want to stop displaying your full last name, so you contact Facebook. At first, this is only a request. Facebook will email you to verify any name requests. It is easy to change this information on Facebook.

Steps to Change Your Name on Facebook Table 2.A
➤ Login → Select Account → Select Settings Tab ➤ Type in new name under Change Name → Click Change Name

Of course, everyone wants to be popular on Facebook and the tips and tricks in *Facebook Fanatic* will help get you there. If you really want to make it easier for old friends to find you on Facebook, use your full last name.

3. Your Password and Security Question

Your Facebook password is obviously very important to your privacy. Never give it out to anyone. Period. Your password must be at least six characters. Using a longer password is better and so is one that combines both letters and numbers. Do not use passwords that are easy to guess like "password" or your name or your pet's name or your birthdate.

Steps to Change Your Password on Facebook Table 2.B
➤ Login → Select Account ➤ In the Settings section type in old password and new password ➤ Confirm new password → Click Change Password

Your security question is nearly as important as your password. Pick one that is also hard to guess. Keep in mind that if someone is trying to gain access to your profile and cannot guess your password they will try to guess your security question. The only safeguard is that Facebook emails the password to you. That way the person trying to gain access still won't learn your password unless they can access your contact email account you've established on Facebook. Many people choose their mother's maiden name as their security question, but this is also one of the easiest to guess since that information can be learned by a quick Internet genealogy search.

Steps to Change Your Security Question on Facebook Table 2.C
➤ Login → Select Account → In Settings section pick security question ➤ Type in the answer → Click Change Security Question

4. Age

Let's be honest, not all information on Facebook is truthful. This may be especially true in the age category! Do not worry. Whether you are young or old, you can always hide your age on Facebook. You must be at least 13 years old to sign up for Facebook. If you suspect there is information on Facebook about any child under 13, contact Facebook at info@facebook.com. As stated above, it is also recommended that you only disclose the first letter of your last name if you are younger than 21.

Steps to Change Your Age on Facebook **Table 2.D**
➢ Login to your profile ➢ Select Edit ➢ In the Basic section change the date and month of your birth ➢ Click Save Changes

You can easily hide your birthdate on Facebook by clicking on Edit → Basic → selecting under Birthday how you want it displayed on your profile → Save Changes.

Once you set your birth year it cannot be changed on Facebook. No cheating!

5. School and Work Networks

The schools you attend(ed) and places you work(ed) are considered networks within Facebook. This means that if you input data into these sections upon signing up, others in these networks such as current and former students (school network) and current and former employees (work network) can view your profile and try to contact you. If you were not aware of this when registering, you can remove yourself from these networks.

Steps to Drop a Network on Facebook **Table 2.E**
➢ Login to your profile → Select Edit → Pick either Education tab or Work tab ➢ Erase inputted data → Click Save Changes

CLASS YEAR COULD REVEAL AGE

If you fibbed about your real age, keep in mind that inputting the year you attended a high school could give away your real age. The same, of course, applies to college.

6. Profile Accessibility

The accessibility of your profile is fundamental to your privacy. Only Facebookers in one of your networks (Region, School or Work), or a friend can access your profile. This is the default privacy

NoteSafety.com is another good privacy information resource.

setting on Facebook. Third party search engines such as Ask.com can also be used to search on your name, network names, photo, and certain profile data such as the number of posts to The Wall. Note that Facebookers who see your limited information in search results will be unable to view your profile unless they are in one of your networks, or a friend. From there you can lock down your profile even more under the My Privacy link.

Users Who Can View Your Facebook Profile Table 2.F
➢ Direct friends (default is full contact information access) ➢ Facebookers who have joined your school, region, or work networks (default is limited contact information access)

Everyone on Facebook should be selective about who they befriend. Remember these are only cyber-friends and you shouldn't tell your life story to them. You may only want to add friends that you know in the physical world. To secure who can view your profile, click on Privacy → Profile. You will then have three privacy options with "All my networks and all my friends" being the default.

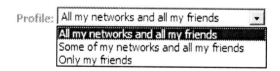

Profile: All my networks and all my friends
All my networks and all my friends
Some of my networks and all my friends
Only my friends

ALWAYS SIGN OUT OF FACEBOOK

Click logout (in the upper right-hand corner) when finished on Facebook. This will protect your privacy, especially if the Internet terminal is in a public place such as a library or school where others will have control of your account if you forget to logout. Even if you click over to another site and then leave the Internet terminal, one click of the browser's "back" button will return a stranger to your Facebook account.

For parental reading, there is a fine guide by privacy attorney Parry Aftab at wiredsafety.org/internet101/Notes.html.

a. Blocking Profile Views

Have you found an annoying person in one of your networks? Got an old girlfriend you want to appear invisible to on Facebook? No problem. Just block them!

Steps to Block a Person on Facebook Table 2.G
➢ Login to your profile → Select Privacy in upper right-hand corner ➢ Under Block People, input person's name or search and add to blocked list

When you block a person on Facebook not only will they be unable to view your profile, but they will also be unable to even search for you to see if you are on Facebook in the first place. They will also be unable to contact you on Facebook.

ANYONE CAN BE BLOCKED

Keep in mind, however, that if a person has learned your email address and you block them, they can always email you outside of Facebook.

All relationship ties you have with the person you block will also be broken. This means the friendship link, and all privileges that go with it, will be severed.

b. Directly Limiting Profile Access

Let's say your ex-boyfriend is on Facebook and even though you have broken up, you remain friends. It is reasonable to perhaps not give your ex full access to your profile. On Facebook this is easy. You can limit profile access to anyone and here is how.

Steps to Limit Profile Access on Facebook Table 2.H
➢ Login to your profile → Select Privacy in upper right-hand corner ➢ Under limited Profile, input person's name or search for them and add them ➢ Select the portions of your profile that will be limited access to them

Even parents of Facebookers cannot have access to their child's account. Facebook states that federal and most state laws forbid it from giving access to a person's account without their permission . . . even to a parent.

PRIVACY & TERMS OF SERVICE   -24-

D. Contact Information and Privacy

An overriding danger with minors not setting their profile to private as shown above is that a predator could befriend them. On Facebook contact information is divulged to direct friends and their direct friends as the default setting. This includes instant messaging screen names,

If a Facebook Member is abusing the service, report them by visiting their profile and clicking on "Report Abuse".

email addresses, phone numbers and home address. Parents may want to become an online friend of their minor children to monitor them online, although kids may not be too happy about this. Below we will learn how to enable key privacy settings for contact information. These are not (as one would intuitively think) found under the Privacy link, but rather by logging into your profile → clicking on Edit → clicking on Contact. Last, the default setting on Facebook is that only friends can view contact information.

1. Email Privacy and Changes

Your email address is an important piece of the personal information pie. There is some confusion as to how email addresses are used on Facebook. The default is that only friends can view your email address. Internally, Facebook will use your email when sending out notifications to you and to verify you are who you say you are. You can change your email address on Facebook at any time. Table 2.I shows the six easy steps on how to do it.

Steps to Change Contact Email Address on Facebook
Table 2.I
➢ Login → Select Account
➢ Under Contact Email click the radio next to "Enter a new email address"
➢ Input new address → Click on Change Contact Email

It's important to lock down your email address from unwanted communications. This will not only protect you from contact by undesirable people, but also from spam email lists. To access your email settings login to your profile → Edit → Contact → Only My Friends next your email address. Pick the desired privacy setting and click Save.

Be wary of the "Find Your Friends" option. What this application does is compile a list of the email addresses you have contacted outside of Facebook. This will include your Granny, people at work, ex-lovers, and perhaps even the company you cursed for spamming you. Do you really want all these people knowing you are on Facebook? Think twice about using this feature as a mass email will be sent out to *all* of them.

2. IM Screen name Privacy

You have three options for instant messaging screen name privacy on Facebook. Note that unlike your email address, you cannot select "Only me" or "No one" as a privacy option. Here the most rigid setting is the default setting, which only allows friends to have access to your IM screen name.

3. Mobile Phone Privacy

Facebook even lets you set the privacy parameters for your cellphone number. Just like with IM screen name privacy, you only have three options and the default is that only your friends can view your cellphone number. This is the tightest privacy option also.

4. Landline Privacy

Lots of people don't use landlines any longer since cellphones are so portable and economical. If you have a landline number in Facebook, however, you have the same three privacy options as you do with IM screen name and cellphone privacy. The default once again is that only your friends can view your landline phone number.

5. Home Address Privacy

Your physical address is very import to your privacy. Do not input it on Facebook unless it is absolutely necessary. Do you really need to get snail-mail from your friends when they likely have five much quicker ways to contact you? You should also not put in your hometown or even your zip code if you are a minor. If you inputted this information upon sign up, you can delete it at any time.

Steps to Change Home Address on Facebook Table 2.J
➢ Login to your profile → Select Edit
➢ Erase old address and input new address → Click Save Changes

You are also given three privacy options for your home address if you feel compelled to include it on Facebook. The default is that only friends can see your address. It is not recommended, but you can also broaden this setting to let a select few of your networks to view your address or all of your networks and all or your friends.

6. Website Privacy

If you have a Website apart from Facebook, you can display the URL so visitors can click over to it via hyperlink. This area also has the three standard privacy settings that we have seen above, but there is a twist. The default here is that all your networks and all your friends can view this link. This makes sense because Websites are publicly available on the Internet. Be careful that you do not divulge private information on your Website that you might not want all Facebookers to see! Locking down your Facebook profile does not mean you have secured all information about you on the Internet.

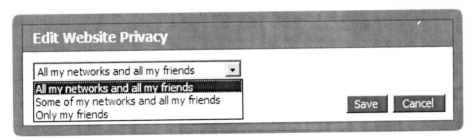

E. Profile Feature Privacy

From your friends, to your photos, to The Wall, you can manually set who has access to these features and much more on your profile. Below we'll discuss each. To reach these key privacy settings login → Privacy → Profile.

1. Friends

Who can see your friends on your profile? There are three privacy options here. "All my networks and all my friends" is the default. Keep in mind that this obviously applies only to Facebookers who can see your profile in the first place (friends, region, school or work networks).

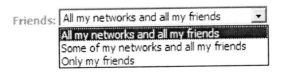

FRIEND OR FOE?

Regardless of how restrictive you make your Facebook privacy settings, your friends will still have access to about 90% of your profile. Keep this in mind before just accepting anyone as your friend.

If you accept a friend invitation from a stranger or person you only know tangentially, be sure to only allow them limited profile access.

2. Tagged Photos, Videos and Notes

On Facebook, photos can be tagged, which means you can identify your friends in the photo so that visitors know who they are and can click on a hyperlink to view them. You can also tag friends in Notes when you use their name in the text. Unlike friends' privacy, you are given an extra option here so that only you can view your own photo tags. Below are the other options with "All my networks and all my friends" being the default.

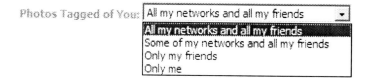

On the opposite end, only your friends can tag you in photos, videos and Notes. Keep in mind that the privacy settings above do not prevent your friends from tagging you in photos, it only disables the hyperlink that allows Facebookers to view more photos of you on your profile. Under the default settings if friends tag a photo of you they have uploaded on your profile, it will also be displayed on your own profile. This could get very embarrassing depending on the photo. As always, you can view your own tagged photos at any time.

BE CAREFUL OF PHOTO CLOTHES

Do not show personal information in photos such as a T-shirt with a school name, phone number, name, address, email address, Website URL, etc.

When you find a photo on Facebook that violates its Terms of Service, you can report it by clicking on "Report this Photo" link beneath it. On the other hand, if a friend (only friends can tag you in photos) has tagged you in an embarrassing photo, you can remove the tag by clicking on the photo and selecting "Remove Tag" adjacent your name. The tag will disappear. Since only friends can tag you in photos, you can remove a person as your friend if they continue to tag you in embarrassing photos. It's that easy.

3. Posts to Your Profile

Many people do not want everyone in their networks (this could include school teachers and ex-friends) to view posts on their profile. No problem. Just select one of the four privacy options below. As with all profile feature privacy settings, "All my networks and all my friends" is the default.

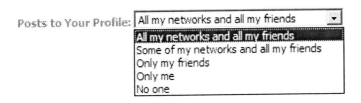

Also be aware that if you select "No one", you will not even be able to see the Posted Items on your own profile! Last, if you stumble across an objectionable post of another person on Facebook, just select the "Report" link beneath the post to let Facebook know about it.

4. Wall

Think of The Wall as your profile's white board where friends can post audio, video and text comments, and check in with you. The Wall is so flexible you can even post messages on it.

Remember, only your friends can post on your Wall. Facebookers in your networks who are not your friends cannot post on The Wall. Your privacy settings dictate who can view The Wall. Once again the default is that everyone can view your Wall.

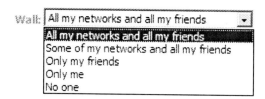

"SEE ALL" AND THE WALL PRIVACY

Be aware that even if the last few postings on The Wall have been innocuous, a visitor merely has to click on "See All" to view all posting to The Wall. This includes potential employers and school administrators.

You can delete postings on The Wall at any time by clicking "delete" next to the post. If a friend continues to place unwanted postings on your Wall, just remove them as a friend and they will be unable to post. Then go back and delete the objectionable postings.

5. Groups

The groups a person belongs to are very personal for some people. You can belong to a maximum of 200 groups and have the option of setting group privacy so that no one can see the groups you belong to when visiting your profile. This comes in handy for motorcycle riders who belong to groups about frilly dresses.

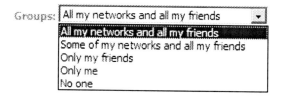

STILL VISIBLE IN GROUP PROFILES

No matter how secure you set your group privacy settings on your profile, keep in mind that you will still be visible on the group itself unless the group settings are set to *secret*.

All newly created groups have a default public setting, which means anyone can read posts and join the group. If you are part of a public group you can still prevent your comments from showing up on your profile's Mini-Feed. Select Privacy → News Feed and Mini-Feed → uncheck "Comment on a Posted Item" and "Leave a Group" boxes. Remember to click Save before leaving. If you are starting a new group and want it to be very private, designate it as secret from the start. If you come across a group that violates Facebook's terms of service, you can anonymously report it by clicking on "Report Group" under the group's photo.

6. Online Status

If you are surfing Facebook during school hours, it is probably a good idea to hide your online status. You may also be studying for finals and simply don't want to be bothered by messages from friends. Pick from one of the four privacy options.

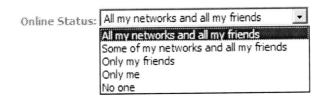

7. Status Updates

Status updates allow you to inform friends what you are doing at this very second. This comes in handy when you are seeing a great movie at the theatre or attending a cool music concert. Now you can even send Facebook status updates to friends' cellphones. With status updates you have three privacy settings and you can never turn status updates off entirely.

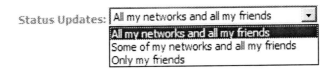

BE CAREFUL ON STATUS UPDATES

If you allow anyone in your networks to see status updates, never give the exact location of where you are to prevent stalking, etc. Status updates can present privacy issues.

8. Flyers

Flyers are mini-ads that are affordable for anyone to run on Facebook. Occasionally an objectionable Flyer will be shown that violates Facebook's Terms of Use. You can report a Flyer by emailing Facebook at the following address: flyers@facebook.com. Be sure to explain in detail why the Flyer in question is objectionable.

9. Notes

Notes are Facebook's version of a Blog. We've already pointed out that BlogSafety.org is an excellent site to get privacy tips in this area. If you come across an objectionable Note posted on Facebook, you can report it by clicking on "Report this Note" beneath the text or photo. There are three main privacy areas for Notes. The first is who can view the Notes you post. If you select that no one can see your Notes, not even you will be able to see them on your profile. The default is that all your networks and friends can view Notes. The other privacy options are the same as for Online Status.

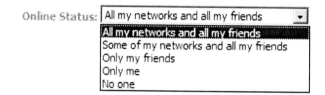

The second privacy area dictates who may comment about the Notes you post. The default here is that anyone who can see your Notes can comment on them. You can ratchet the privacy up a notch by only allowing your friends to comment on Notes. Last, you can disallow comments completely for the highest level of privacy.

The third privacy section for Facebook Notes is Syndication. This covers who can subscribe to your Notes so that they will be fed to their profile. The default setting again is that anyone who can see your Notes can subscribe to them. The other privacy setting disables subscriptions to your Notes totally.

10. Marketplace

If you post an item for sale on Facebook Marketplace, you must still keep privacy in mind. Never include your address or phone number in your posting. If a person is interested in your item, they can message you. In this regard, also be aware that you can opt to have your Marketplace ad shown in all networks. That means people will be able to message you who are not in your regular networks.

When you do get an item inquiry, try not to give out your home contact info if at all possible. Of course, if you are selling a bedroom suite the buyer will need to see it. If you must let a stranger view an item (or pick up an item) at your home, be sure to not be there by yourself. Have friends there to help. It's best to meet strangers at public places such as parks or libraries to complete the transaction if they must see the item first. If the item is mailable, this is the preferred method of getting the item to strangers. Ensure, of course, that they have paid for it first through a secure third party site such as PayPal.com.

11. Videos

Facebook Video privacy is even more important in many ways than photo and Note privacy because moving pictures and audio voices are involved, which usually means they tell much more of the story. You begin adding privacy settings when you decide to add the Facebook Video application to your profile. Stories about

> If Facebookers can see your video anywhere on Facebook, they can comment on it. Keep that in mind and monitor your comments periodically to delete undesirable ones.

when you publish new videos can be shown in News Feed and Mini-Feed if you would like. You also select whether a link to your profile will be set when viewed on other profiles.

The default option is that both of these are set. If you are frightened that you may see objectionable matter on the Video application across Facebook, be sure to click "Block Video" in the lower right-hand corner of the add Video application screen. For each Video that you create you will have the option of picking a unique privacy setting for that video. The default is that everyone on Facebook, regardless of what networks to which they belong, will be able to watch your video.

Apart from the default privacy setting, you can limit those who can view your videos to only those who can see your profile (i.e., those in your networks), your friends and the friends of those you have tagged in your video, or only your friends.

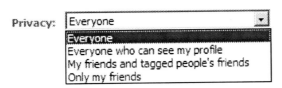

F. Search Privacy

There is some initial confusion over search privacy on Facebook. If you login → click on Privacy → Search, you can change the privacy settings for searches conducted within Facebook itself. This begs the question: How can Facebookers search for you on Facebook? They can search on your name (remember that if you only put the first letter of your last name, your full last name will not be searchable), or any part of your name.

Let's say you go to a small school and have a distinctive first name. If a person remembers your distinctive first name they can easily find you by searching.

<u>ANYONE CAN SEARCH FOR YOU</u>

Anyone can search for you on Facebook, but once they find you, they must be in one of your networks (friend, school, region or work) to view your profile.

What happens when a long lost person finds you, but is not in one of your networks? They will still be able to see your profile photo in the search results and name. They can also message you, poke you, and send you a friend request. This is the default and we will see below how to change this. To prevent access by potential predators, minors should not respond to any stranger who tries to contact them in this way.

1. Who Can Find You in Search Results

Okay. We've learned the default on Facebook is that anyone can search for you. You can, however, tighten privacy here by selecting one of the other three setting options. At all times friends will be able to search for you.

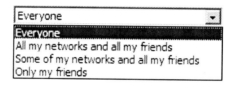

If the above controls above weren't enough, you can allow Facebookers in certain networks to search for you.

2. What People Can Do With Your Search Results

If you don't want people to be able to see your profile photo in the search results, message you, poke you, and send you a friend request, then uncheck the desired boxes below. Minors should uncheck all of these.

3. Search Engine Privacy Case Study

No section on Facebook privacy would be complete without discussing whether search engines can find your profile from outside of Facebook. And if they can, what information is revealed to the world? Below is an Ask.com search case study on the founder of Facebook, Mark Zuckerberg.

The results that were served by Ask.com were uneventful. Of course, many articles about Mr. Zuckerberg appeared in the search results, but his profile, which is private, was not revealed. The same applied to a Google search. Facebook has done a good job keeping its profiles from the peering eyes of public search engines on the Internet. If people are searching for you on Facebook, they will likely perform a search like the one demonstrated above. If you don't want to be found by public search engines, yet want to avoid the Facebook privacy restriction for search, ensure that you are not using your full last name. In addition, keep the word "Facebook" out of the body of your profile as most people will search on this term when checking for your Facebook profile. If a person is using their full last name, type the following into your browser and replace "mark +zuckerberg" with the first and last name of the person in question http://www.facebook.com/s.php?q=mark+zuckerberg. You must be logged into Facebook for this to work. Alternatively, you can visit a person's profile on Facebook. Copy and paste the URL to return to the profile at a latter time. Note, you must be logged in to Facebook to see this page after copying and pasting the URL into your browser window. Here is the URL for Mark Zuckerberg's profile on Facebook: http://www.facebook.com/networks/?nk=50431648. Last, each Facebook profile has another URL that includes your username and a unique profile ID.

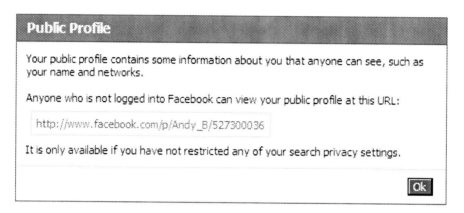

G. News Feed and Mini-Feed

The News Feed and Mini-Feed applications were controversial when first launched. Facebook quickly added a number of privacy features that calmed most people's concerns. If you are not familiar with these two applications, News Feed updates what profile changes you have made on your friends' profiles and likewise, their changes are fed to your profile. Isn't that digital cannibalism? ;) Mini-Feed shows updates you've made on your own profile for those who may be visiting.

Not only that, but with Mini-Feed a person can click on "See All" to see *every* change you have ever made on your profile! This can raise privacy issues for some. At first it is confusing as to what is published on News Feed and Mini-Feed and what is not. So here is a breakdown.

Information that May be Published on News Feed & Mini-Feed	Information Never Published on News Feed & Mini-Feed
➤ Additions to Profile	➤ Events You Decline
➤ Content Posted to Profile	➤ Friend Requests You Reject
➤ Events Attended or Created	➤ Friends You Remove
➤ Groups Joined or Created	➤ Groups You Decline to Join
➤ Networks Joined	➤ Messages Sent

➢ Notes Written	➢ Notes Deleted
➢ Notes You're Tagged in	➢ Notes Read – by Whom
➢ Photos You're Tagged in	➢ Photos Deleted
➢ Photos Uploaded	➢ Photos Viewed – by Whom
➢ Status Updates	➢ Pokies & Whose Profiles Viewed

1. Publish Stories When I . . .

If you want to prevent Facebook from publishing a newsflash when you do any of the things below, just uncheck the appropriate boxes. As a default, all boxes are checked.

2. Show Times of Stories

News Feed and Mini-Feed automatically post the times of your profile changes and this is the default setting. To turn it off just uncheck the box below and remember to click on Save Changes before you return to your profile.

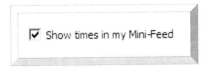

TURN OFF TIMES IF USING AT WORK OR SCHOOL
If you are brave enough to use Facebook at work or school, do not show the times in News Feed or Mini-Feed or risk losing your job when a co-worker visits your profile.

You can delete any Mini-Feed story on your profile by clicking the x in the upper corner. Remember that you are always in control on Facebook.

H. Poke, Message and Friend Request
The three ways you can contact potential new friends on Facebook are by sending a friend request, shooting a message or poking them. When you do this, Facebook lets the potential new friend see key profile information of yours so that they can adequately determine whether you are the type of person whom they want to befriend. The default areas of your profile they can see are: basic and education info, your friends, personal info, photos in which you are tagged, posts, and work info. You add to or disable viewing of this default profile information by checking the appropriate boxes.

USE THE PREVIEW FEATURE
Next to the profile information check boxes is a preview of what your profile will look like to invitees. Ensure the information shown is the right amount before clicking Save.

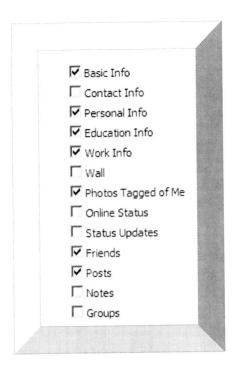

Are you one of those who send friend requests on such a frequent basis that you forget to whom you have sent them? If so, Facebook provides a helpful list in the lower right-hand corner of this section. It displays people to whom you have sent friend invites, messages, poked and prodded.

I. Notes
Blogs = Notes on Facebook. If you have used Blogs on other social networking sites, such as MySpace or Bebo, you will be off to the races with Notes. As with your other profile areas, there are key privacy settings of which you need to be aware.

1. Access
Your profile notes can be very private or very public. The choice is up to you, but be aware that the default is that everyone (including those not in your networks) can see your notes.

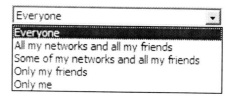

ONLY ME?

The Only Me privacy setting for Notes is not as tight as it seems. Anyone you tag in your Notes can also view them. The lesson is: Don't put tags in your Notes if you are maintaining them as a personal journal online.

2. Note Comments

Do you want Facebookers commenting on your Notes? If you don't trust your friends, or if they are practical jokers, you may want to prevent their comments. If so, you do not have to do anything as this is the default privacy setting. Also keep in mind that if you allow anyone to read your Notes (default setting) and pick the least private comments setting, then anyone on Facebook can comment on them.

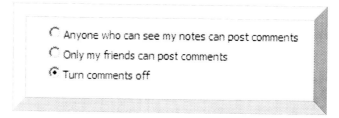

3. Subscribership

You can also set who can subscribe to your Notes. When a person subscribes they will receive new updates you make to your profile Notes. The default is that no one can subscribe, but if you pick the first setting, and you let any one Facebook read your Notes, then anyone can subscribe.

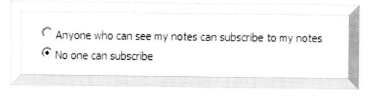

J. Facebook Platform

Call them widgets, gizmos, or whatever you want, Facebook allows developers, through the Facebook Platform, to create applications such as Facebook Toolbar for Firefox, Your Hottest Friend, and Facebook Exporter for iPhoto. Below are the privacy settings that apply to Facebook Platform applications. In particular, the *checked* items will divulge information from your profile to the applications to which you have granted access. The default settings are set forth below.

☑ Profile picture

☑ Basic info What's this?

☑ Personal info (activities, interests, etc.)

☑ Current location (what city you're in)

☑ Education history

☑ Work history

☑ Profile status

☑ Wall

☑ Notes

☑ Groups you belong to

☑ Events you're invited to

☑ Photos taken by you

☑ Photos taken of you

☑ Relationship status

☐ What type of relationship you're looking for

☐ What sex you're interested in

☐ Who you're in a relationship with

☐ Religious views

ADDITIONAL INFORMATION SHARED

Checking *any* item above will also divulge your profile name, list of friends and networks to the application. Since third parties create many of these, this can have an effect on your privacy. Outside applications, however, may not store your data. Facebook also will never sell your data.

K. Facebook Terms of Service

If you are okay with the privacy of your information on Facebook, you must also ensure that you agree with its Terms of Service: http://www.facebook.com/terms.php. As we've discussed, Facebook does not allow anyone under the age of 13 to access its site. You also cannot solicit personal information from anyone under 18 or register for more than one account.

1. Information and Copying It

All information submitted to Facebook must be truthful and non-offensive. What's more, Facebook must not be used commercially and you cannot collect email address from Facebook to be used commercially. The information on the site can be downloaded or printed, but intellectual property notices such as copyright and trademark symbols must remain at all times.

2. Facebook's Liability Limitations

At any time Facebook can refuse or remove any posting. It can restrict access to any area without cause. Facebook limits its liability for using the service to $1000 or the amount you have paid to use the service (hint: Facebook is free). All disputes will be decided in arbitration. The laws of the State of Delaware govern the Terms of Service.

3. Your Intellectual Property

The term "intellectual property" covers everything from copyrights (written text, video, photos, etc.) to patents. You retain ownership to all videos, Notes material, photos, etc. that you upload to Facebook. It does, however, take "an irrevocable, perpetual, non-exclusive, transferable, fully paid, worldwide license (with the right to sublicense) to use, copy, publicly perform, publicly display, reformat, translate, excerpt (in whole or in part) and distribute such User Content for any purpose on or in connection with the Site or the promotion thereof, to prepare derivative works of, or incorporate into other works, such User Content, and to grant and authorize sublicenses of the foregoing. You may remove your User Content from the Site at any time. If you choose to remove your User Content, the license granted above will automatically expire." Copyrights on Facebook and their violations are governed by the Digital Millenium Copyright Act. Here are the particulars if you need to report a violation.

DMCA Needed Info	DMCA Facebook Contact
Name of Agent Designated to Receive Notification of Claimed Infringement	Rudy Gadre
Full Address of Designated Agent to Which Notification Should be Sent	156 University Ave., Suite 300 Palo Alto, CA 94301
Telephone Number of Designated Agent	(650) 543-4800
Facsimile Number of Designated Agent	(650) 543-4801
E-Mail Address of Designated Agent	copyright@facebook.com

Here is what Facebook requires when submitting a notification under the DMCA. "To meet the notice requirements under the Digital Millennium Copyright Act, the notification must be a written communication that includes the following:

A. physical or electronic signature of a person authorized to act on behalf of the owner of an exclusive right that is allegedly infringed;

B. Identification of the copyrighted work claimed to have been infringed, or, if multiple copyrighted works at a single online site are covered by a single notification, a representative list of such works at that site;

C. Identification of the material that is claimed to be infringing or to be the subject of infringing activity and that is to be removed or access to which is to be disabled, and information reasonably sufficient to permit us to locate the material;

D. Information reasonably sufficient to permit us to contact the complaining party, such as an address, telephone number and, if available, an electronic mail address at which the complaining party may be contacted;

E. A statement that the complaining party has a good-faith belief that use of the material in the manner complained of is not authorized by the copyright owner, its agent or the law; and

F. A statement that the information in the notification is accurate, and under penalty of perjury, that the complaining party is authorized to act on behalf of the owner of an exclusive right that is allegedly infringed."

L. Facebook Platform Terms of Service

Most of us want to use those groovy little applications that developers code for Facebook. They let you do cool things to your profile like rate your hottest friends and import pictures directly from iPhoto into Facebook. Because most of these applications are developed by third parties outside of Facebook, special terms of service apply that can affect your privacy on Facebook.

For starters, Facebook must allow these developers access to certain information on your profile for the applications to work on what is called the Facebook Development Platform (FBDP). The following list displays information available from your profile to the Facebook Development Platform.

Information Available to FBDP	Information Not Available to FBDP
➢ Birthday	➢ Email Address
➢ Gender	➢ Instant Message ID
➢ Interests	➢ Street Address
➢ Location	➢ Telephone Number
➢ Name	➢ Website (Personal)
➢ Networks to Which You Belong	
➢ Photos (Default & Albums)	
➢ Political Views	
➢ Number of Friends	
➢ Number of Messages	
➢ Number of Pokes	
➢ User ID	

60 Second Summary

Key Privacy & Terms of Service Tips

- Must be 13 or older to use Facebook
- Be sure to make your profile private if under 18
- Use first letter of last name if under 21
- You cannot change birth year once inputted
- The default on Facebook is that anyone can search for you
- Never give out your password
- Don't show your apartment, home or school in Facebook photos
- Be friend selective
- You own your intellectual property and Facebook has a limited license
- Facebook information can be downloaded or printed, but intellectual property notices such as trademark symbols and copyright notices must remain
- Facebook's copyright violations are governed under the Digital Millennium Copyright Act
- Know what information you are giving away by using Facebook Applications

What You'll Experience

First and Last Names

Learning Your URL

Name Limitations

Adding Facebook URL to Emails

III   Facebook URL

A. Facebook URL Introduction

Your screen name on Facebook is merely your first and last names (or first letter of your last name). Your name is used to set your unique Facebook URL.

NAME LIMITATIONS

Since your screen name becomes part of a Facebook URL, it carries with it all the limitations of a domain name. This means it is limited to the English characters A-Z, numbers 0-9, the hyphen -, and the underscore _ mark.

Your Facebook URL is formed from your chosen name and a unique number identifier. This is often called "Your Facebook" as in someone asking you: "What's your Facebook?" It is the "Facebook URL" to be perfectly clear. Here is an example of Mark Zuckerberg's Facebook URL: http://www.facebook.com/p/Mark_Zuckerberg/50431648.

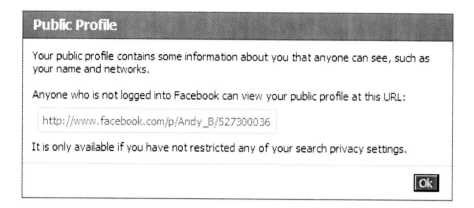

Your Facebook profile is nothing more than a Website under the Facebook umbrella. It therefore must be unique. The shorter and more succinct, the easier your Facebook URL is to remember. You can also add a nickname after your first name such as "Anna 'shorty' Brown" or "Carl 'The Face' Smith". When you type in your first name, add the nickname in single quotes right after it.

FACEBOOK URL NOT SET IN STONE

Since you can change your Facebook name and it is part of your URL, your URL can also change. This will make it harder for people to find you who may have it stored in their favorites within their Internet browser.

B. Adding Facebook URL to Email Messages

Your Facebook URL can easily be added to outgoing email messages in the form of a hyperlink that your non-Facebook friends can click on to be taken to your profile. Below is an example with everything from the http to just before the first > being the Facebook profile URL.

Put a link to your Facebook profile on AIM:
<a href=http://www.facebook.com/p/Andy_B/527300036>Facebook me!</a>

1. Add Facebook URL to AIM Info Box

Once you have created a cool Facebook profile, you have to tell everyone about it. AOL Instant Messenger allows you to attach information to your screen name so that people you IM can read your information even when you are not online. This is your AIM calling card and you can easily provide a hyperlink to your Facebook profile using it.

Hyperlink Facebook URL Via AIM Info Box Table 3.A
➢ Log into AIM → Select My AIM from the toolbar → Pick Edit Profile
➢ Click on Next until you reach the More Info screen
➢ Paste this HTML code into the window: <font face="Times New Roman" size="4">Check out what I've got on Facebook <a href=[FACEBOOK URL] target="_blank">Facebook!</a></font>
➢ Click on Finish and you are all set

2. Add Facebook URL to Gmail Signatures

Link your Facebook profile automatically to your Gmail messages.

Hyperlink Facebook URL to Gmail Signatures Table 3.B
➢ Log into Gmail account → Pick Settings from top of profile
➢ Paste this HTML code into the Signature box: Check out what I've got on Facebook at [FACEBOOK URL]
➢ Click the radio button next to the Signature box
➢ Hit Save Changes at the bottom of the screen and you are finished

3. Add Facebook URL to Hotmail Signatures

Hyperlink your Facebook profile automatically to your Hotmail messages.

Hyperlink Facebook URL to Hotmail Signatures **Table 3.C**
➢ Log into Hotmail account → Pick Options from right-hand side of profile
➢ Select Mail from left-hand side of profile → Click on Personal Signature
➢ Paste this HTML code into the box: Check out what I've got on Facebook at [FACEBOOK URL] → Click OK and you are all set

4. Add Facebook URL to Yahoo Mail Signatures

Link your Facebook profile automatically to Yahoo Mail messages.

Hyperlink Facebook URL to Yahoo Mail Signatures **Table 3.D**
➢ Log into Yahoo Mail account → Pick Options from right-hand side of profile
➢ Select Signature under the Management column
➢ Paste this HTML code into the box: Check out what I've got on Facebook at [FACEBOOK URL]
➢ Click box next to "Add signature to all outgoing messages"
➢ Click Save in the lower left corner and you are finished

You can also add images of yourself and emoticons to your emails. Here is a list of four top sites to further add some zip to your emails.

Email Images of Yourself **Table 3.E**
➢ Blingee.com
➢ Iconator.com
➢ ImageChef.com
➢ MyTextGraphics.com

60 Second Summary

Key URL Tips
• Name limited to characters A-Z, 0-9, - and _
• First and Last name are incorporated into Facebook URL
• You can change your name, but this will also change your URL
• It's easy to add a URL profile hyperlink to outgoing Facebook messages

What You'll Experience

Eight Profile Interests

Quotes and More Quotes

Make Custom Interest Sections

Buzz Your Book & Movie Sections

IV   Interests

A. Eight Profile Interests

Within your profile are eight interest sections you can fill with all sorts of info about your likes and dislikes. These areas are one of the best ways for Facebookers to get to know you. To modify them click on Edit → Personal tab. Below you will learn the tips and tricks to getting the most out of these sections and how to make your profile shine.

INSERT HYPERLINKS IN ANY INTEREST SECTION

Got a cool new Website you want to tell the world about? Just type the address into any interest section. You do not need all that http:// or even the www in front of the domain name. A simple bottletreebooks.com works fine.

1. About

The About interest section is very important as this is the first information Facebookers usually read about you. It is listed near the top of your Facebook profile. It should grab attention and summarize how you want to be known on Facebook. Tell your history like no one else can.

The About section is not limited in characters so tell as much information about yourself as you want, but keep it interesting.

Tell them where you have been and where you are going. It's okay to brag. Really, it is. Take the opportunity to extend your profile's theme. If you are a fledgling poet, tell about your favorite poets here; or better yet, type out one of your own short poems or sonnets! Are you a Harley rider? If so, tell about your favorite Harley Davidson motorcycles. Are you a baller? Let Facebookers know about your favorite basketball team. You get the picture. Remember that your Facebook profile should reflect your theme in most all areas. Your Facebook photo is your first theme introduction and your About section the second.

REMEMBER TO CLICK "SAVE"

Way down at the bottom of the page beneath the Personal tab is the Save button. Remember to click it so your interest changes take effect on your profile.

Tip

A great way to spice up *any* interest section is to add symbols to your text. That's right. You can use non-standard characters when typing in your interest section. One of the best ways to go about this is to use symbols from a word processing program like Microsoft Word and then copy and paste them into your profile.

Inserting Microsoft Word Symbols Table 4.A
➢ Launch Word → Open a new file → Click Insert from the top file menu
➢ Select Symbols → Pick your symbols and click Insert
➢ Close the symbol window
➢ Copy and paste symbols into your interest section under Edit → Personal tab

2. Favorite Music

If you're part of music fan clubs outside of Facebook, list the URLs in the favorite music section.

The second interest section is where you can tell the world all about your favorite music. What a great place to start. Most of us can go on for days about the music we like.

This section gives you that chance in spades with unlimited word space. If you like certain bands, tell everybody. But more importantly, tell them *why* you like them. Favorite songs or albums? List them here. Do you have a guitar pick from *U2*'s The Edge? Tell everyone about it.

3. Favorite Movies

It is easy to list your top ten favorite movies of all time, and important, but you can accomplish so much more with this section. Provide URLs that give deeper info about your favorite movies. One of the best sites is the Internet Movie Database that can be found at <u>imdb.com</u>. Find the page for your movie, copy and paste the URL from your browser's window, and link to it under this section.

LINK TO YOUR FAVORITE MOVIE STAR'S WEBSITE
If you love Jack Black movies such as "School of Rock", do not forget to provide a URL to his Website so visitors to your Facebook profile can discover him too.

4. Activities

For all you sports lovers, this is the section to expound on what sports you like playing as well as your favorite teams. If you belong to a school team, let Facebookers know. This interest section is a great place to show your school colors. Link to the official Websites of your favorite teams. Of course the actual title is "Activities" not "Sports" so feel free to list any hobbies you have in this area!

5. Favorite Quotes

This is an excellent section to quote your heroes. Great quotes can get you tons of friends. Two of the best (and free) quote sites on the Internet are <u>wisdomquotes.com</u> and <u>quoteland.com</u>. So go ahead and quote, quote, quote.

QUOTE YOURSELF

Some of the best quotes on Facebook do not come from some politician or musician, but from people like you. So get out there and quote yourself.

6. Interests

This section is closely related to Activities. In short, put your hobbies that don't involve physical action here such as watching movies, reading, going to the theatre to see plays, etc. If you are a book collector, put it here, and if you are a skier, put it in the Activities section. A good idea is to list the people you would like to meet. This is a great way to get to know people that may be one or two steps removed from your circle of friends. For instance, if you want to meet a cheerleader from another school, putting it here and it may get noticed. You are not limited. Put dead people here too! You will never get to meet them (run if they show up at your door), but this will flavor who you are and what you are about. Be creative with this section. It does not have to be limited to people. If you want to meet Bart Simpson from *The Simpsons* cartoon show, put it down. Superheroes are popular in this space as are most *Star Wars* characters.

SPELL CHECK TEXT

Always copy and paste your words into a word processing program such as Microsoft Word so that you can run a spell check before placing the text on your profile. Misspelled words will not help your popularity.

Here is another idea for this section. We all have heroes. These could be as close as a parent, teacher or coach or they may be so far removed that you never knew them but wish you did, such as Jesus Christ. Get creative here and think long and hard about who your heroes are. They certainly do not have to be alive!

7. Favorite Books

This is a very important section. Lots of Facebookers think books aren't cool. Wrong! Books will take you to worlds unknown and let you meet fascinating people. Reading the classics (even if they are only a few decades old) will let you in on the secrets hundreds of thousands of readers already know. At parties and business functions for the rest of your life you will be on the "inside" when a reference is made to the bunch of morons from *Catcher in the Rye* or the temperature at which books burn that is in the title of *Fahrenheit 451*. Plus, Facebook does not limit the amount of words you have available here. By listing your favorite books you will show Facebookers you are cool, not a dweeb. And you will also attract many others who have read and enjoyed the same books. Begin reading today. To get started, here is a list of the top 100 novels from The

Modern Library (randomhouse.com/modernlibrary/100bestnovels.html), the BBC (bbc.co.uk/arts/bigread/top100.shtml), and last but not least, *Time Magazine* (time.com/time/2005/100books/the_complete_list.html). Enjoy!

8. Favorite TV Shows

More and more television shows are being shown online and on portable devices. The speed at which shows are available for download has increased tremendously with the video iPod and iPhone. To enhance the visitor experience on your profile, provide URLs to your favorite shows so that others can download them. Amazon.com's Unbox feature also lets you download shows on its Website: unbox.com.

A great way to see other Facebookers who enjoy the same books, movies and TV shows is to visit your profile and click on any of the automatically generated links for them. This will bring up a search list of other Facebookers who have listed the same item. Be careful of the titles you input. If it is not the correct title of the book, it will not link to other Facebookers. For instance, if you type "My fave AdWords book is Google Advertising Guerrilla Tactics", the entire phrase will be taken as one and will not link to Facebookers who just typed in "Google Advertising Guerrilla Tactics".

60 Second Summary

Key Interests Tips
• Extend your profile's theme • Insert non-standard characters • Link to your favorite sites so other Facebookers can buy your favorites • Quote yourself • Spell check text before adding it

What You'll Experience

Profile Views

Photos A-Z

Photo Captions & Ranking

Automatically Add Photos to Emails

V   **Photo Fantastica**

A. Default Photo

When you first sign up for Facebook you are asked to upload a representative photo of yourself. You have the option to not display a photo and have a big fat question shown in its place, but this will greatly decrease the number of people that will be interested in your profile. When you upload your default photo it appears on your profile instantly and is stuck in a photo album titled "Profile Pictures". A thumbnail of your photo will be shown in the search results along with your profile name.

Your photo is the first introduction Facebookers see, so make it stand out from the others. Click Photos on the left-hand side of your profile to get started. You will also be asked to upload a default photo when you sign up. Keep in mind that Facebook limits photo sizes to 4MB.

First off, get your photo in sync with your profile's theme. If you have a dark themed profile, but a shiny happy photo where you are wearing a T-shirt with a rainbow on it, your profile visits will drop. Say the theme of your profile is snow skiing, but your photo is one you took on family vacation at the beach. This will tank your profile visits. Your photo could be like tens of thousands or even hundreds of thousands of photos, and this sort of generic photo will not increase your friends. How many photos on Facebook are there of two or three people hugging and partying? A hundred thousand? A million? You see these photos all the time. They do not stand out anymore, and make it difficult to tell which one is the person whose Facebook profile you are visiting. Uniqueness is the best way to climb up the Facebook popularity ladder. Of course, being a beautiful girl in a little bikini helps, too. But if that is not your game (and for most of us it is *not*), then make your photo different.

Top Three Reasons for Poor Facebook Photos   **Table 5.A**
➢ Poor image quality   ➢ Does not sync with profile theme   ➢ Photo is not unique

Want to make your profile fresh and exciting? Want to freak out your friends? There is an easy way to do it by using the rotate feature on Facebook. Click on your profile photo and in the lower right you can rotate it in any direction. April Fools day is great day to hang upside down on your Facebook profile.

1. Uploading

Uploading any file on your computer into Facebook to make it your default photo is easy. Below we'll show you the steps. Do not upload a

Facebook allows photos in .jpg, .gif and .png formats.

256 KB photo when you are allowed 4MB clarity. Fuzzy photos will plummet in the ranking system. It is much better to have a clear, close-up than a shot of you in the distance where users cannot make out your face. Squinting is not cool on the Internet, especially on Facebook. If you forego uploading a photo when you first sign up for Facebook, it is easy to upload one at any later time to get rid of the dreaded question mark that is shown in its place.

Steps to Upload a Photo Table 5.B
➤ Select Edit → Click on Picture tab → Browse for photos on your computer ➤ Check box to certify that you own the rights to distribute the photo ➤ Click Upload Picture

2. Sending a Photo

After your photo(s) are uploaded, you are automatically taken to the invite section of your profile and asked to contact all of the people in your email address books on AOL, Gmail, Hotmail, Hotmail.co.uk, Hotmail.ca, MSN and Yahoo.com, Yahoo.ca, and Yahoo.co.uk. The default is your Facebook sign-in email program.

Once you give Facebook your email address and password, its computer algorithms automatically gather your email address book contacts. The list of those on Facebook will appear and you select which to contact. Be sure to delete any friends or relatives from the list that you do not want to receive the invite. Be aware that when you contact friends in your email address books your photo will be attached to your email message.

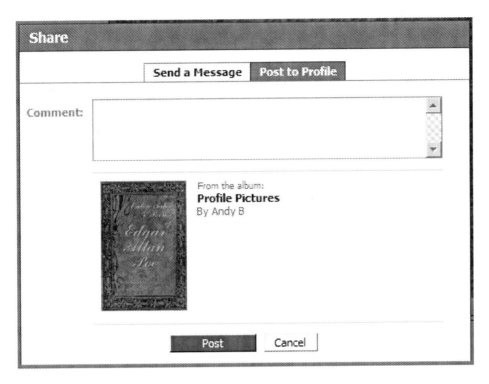

Let's say you see a great photo on Facebook and want to show your friends. No problem. Look below any photo and you will see the Share icon.

What's more, you can always make any photo smaller before emailing it to friends. Have you ever gotten an emailed photo that you have to scroll top to bottom and side to side to see it all? Well here is how to fix that issue for your friends when emailing Facebook photos outside of Facebook.

Resize Photos in Windows Table 5.C
➢ Click Start in lower left-hand corner ➢ Select My Pictures (or any folder where you keep your digital photos) ➢ Click on desired photo → Select "E-mail this file" from the left-hand column

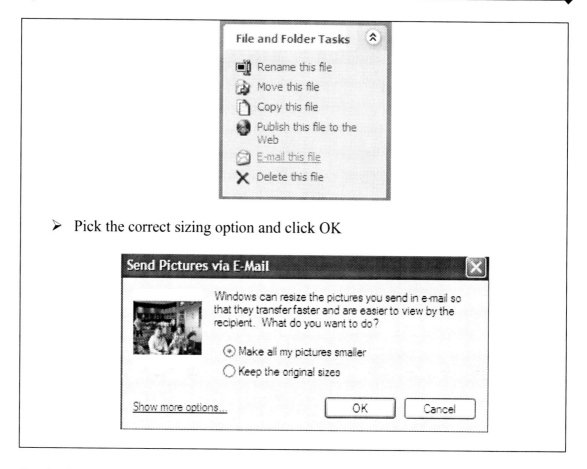

> Pick the correct sizing option and click OK

On the Mac, use the free iPhoto software. Click on any photo and select the email icon near the bottom of the screen. At this point you can pick from a variety of sizing options.

3. Viewing Photos and Comments

To quickly view your Facebook photos click on Photos → My Photos and you will be presented with your photo albums. Click on any to see the pictures inside.

Here you can also view comments about your photos made by friends. If you don't like the comments or agree with them, simply delete them. Note that depending upon the level of access Facebookers have to your profile, they will also be able to read photo comments. This includes your boss at work or teacher.

4. Ordering of Photos

The first photo you upload is automatically your default photo that will be shown when users browse Facebook. You can, however, rearrange your photos to make another one your default at any time.

Steps to Reorder Photos
Table 5.D
➤ Login → Click the Photos tab → Select Photos of Me link → Pick an album
➤ Drag and drop photos to reorder them → Click Save Changes when finished

Change your default photo once in a while. Rotate your default photo based on the amount of traffic you are getting. If you get a hundred visitors a day, you had better upload a lot of new photos to keep people coming back. On the other hand, if you only get a few visitors to your Facebook profile you do not have to rotate them so often. But take it as a hint that you could get more visitors with more/different photos.

Selecting "Reverse Order" when you are in a photo album is a quick and easy way to change your default photo instead of dragging and dropping photos.

So many people on Facebook upload pictures and forget about them. At a minimum, change your photos with the seasons. Unless you live in a climate that is cold year around, visitors do not want to see photos of you in a snow parka during summer!

PHOTO CHANGED ACROSS FRIENDS' PROFILES
When you change your default photo, it will change across the entire Facebook network. That means the new photo will appear on all your friends' profiles and in any comments you have left on The Wall.

You do not even have to show a picture of yourself on Facebook to have a popular profile. There are a lot of faceless and beheaded people on Facebook these days. Has the headless horseman escaped from Sleepy Hollow? Are aliens snatching faces? Naw. A great way to promote your "best asset" is to show it on Facebook. Do you have the world's tallest pair of stiletto heals? Show them! If you have an awesome motocross bike, show that. If dogs rock your world, put a photo of Fido on your profile. If you have great abs, show them. Do you have a rad tattoo? Show it! Wild room? Snap a photo of it. Faces are so 1990s! Once you have a circle of friends you can swap all the face photos you want, but use your best asset to draw them in under your default photo.

Another way to set your default photo apart is to create an avatar of yourself, which is a cartoon-like representation. Copy the .jpg onto your computer and upload to Facebook. That is all there is to it. Here are some top avatar sites.

Top Facebook Avatar Sites Table 5.E
➢ 3b.net
➢ imvu.com
➢ avatars.yahoo.com
➢ gravatar.com
➢ zwinky.com

5. Photo Tags and Comments

Tag you're it! Viewing you friends' photo albums and tagging people in photos is easy. Typically just the name of the person who uploaded the photo is shown below it. If a photo has been tagged, all Facebook names of the people shown in the photo are displayed under the photo. Hovering over any name will highlight the person with a box around their face and clicking on their name will take you to their profile. To get started tagging, click Photos in the left-hand column.

This will default to a view of your friends' photo albums and those that you have recently visited.

Recent Photo Albums

Click on the tab next to "Recent Photo Albums" and this is where you can view friends you have recently tagged.

Recently Tagged Friends

This is a handy feature Facebook provides because friends you take the time to tag are usually important. Likewise, they can tag you in photos and these links will be shown on their profiles. What's more, tagging a person in a photo is easy. When you click on the person a box will highlight them and you can add their name and a description, which is not limited in characters.

Facebook limits photo captions to 100 characters, including spaces. This should be adequate for most photos.

Hovering over a tagged photo will show the text of the tag such as "Mike, Jim and I at Teresa's wedding, April 2007". When you click on the Photos link you have a wealth of photo options at your disposal. You can upload new photos, create a new photo album, view your friend's albums, or tag friends in existing photos. Photo comments are a great way to add information to often-cryptic pictures. You might fully understand the bet you lost that required you to jump around on a pogo stick in your underwear with a cowboy hat on, but your visitors will not. They may even think it is a daily occurrence in your life, so make them understand through tags.

If you have a caption for your default photo it will *not* be seen on your direct profile. Then where, exactly, are they shown? Well, a Facebooker must click on your photo. This will launch a new screen that enlarges your photo. If you have blemishes that you think no one will see on the thumbnail-sized photo, think again. Hovering over the photo will cause the comment to be displayed.

MAKE PHOTOS COMMENTS DESCRIPTIVE

So many Facebook photo captions are cryptic and tell visitors nothing about you, why the photo is on your profile or what you are doing in it. Spend a little time on your captions to make them descriptive. Instead of saying: "Jenny & Craig" write: "2006 Prom – Jenny & Craig." Replace: "Me at NIN" with "NIN Concert, 7/17/06 Miami" so that others who went to the concert can link up with you. More content equals more popularity.

Last, photo comments have attributed to them unlimited characters so don't be shy in this area. Are they searchable in Facebook? No, so you can be a little more forthcoming in them if desired. Also, while you can type URLs into your photo comments, Facebook does not automatically insert a hyperlink so visitors must copy and paste the URL into their browser window to visit the site.

6. Photo Printshop

Printing physical copies of your digital Facebook photos is easy.

Facebook has partnered with QOOP (www.QOOP.com), one of the Internet's leading photo printing services. With QOOP you can order photos, coffee mugs with pictures on them, posters, etc. You name it and QOOP can usually print your photos on it. You can even order books of photos. This is a great way to make your own yearbook of, say, your senior year of college or a photo album of a sports team that can sit on a coffee table for years to come. Below is an example of various print sizes you can order and the price for each.

An important privacy setting for your Facebook photos is to set the parameters for who can print them. Since friends have full access, you need to decide if they can print them out. When they do, you lose a bit of control. The default is that only you can print out photos you have uploaded to Facebook. Click Photos → Photo Printshop link → select privacy setting.

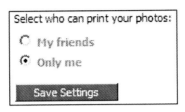

B. Resizing Photos and Thumbnails

There are a number of options when adding photos to your Facebook profile. Your Facebook photo is one of the most important sections of your profile. It can make or break your popularity in a heartbeat. Contrary to popular belief, Facebook photos are not a looks contest. Some of the best looking people have terrible Facebook photos and others, who couldn't buy a date, have great photos and their Facebook profiles are all the rage. Whatever your photo is about, ensure it reflects the *theme* you are trying to convey. Be sure to upload multiple photos on Facebook, too. This is a great way to show different looks on your Facebook profile! Try to match your Facebook photo to your hobby. If you're a surfer, post a photo of you catching a wave or at least one of the cool detailing on your surfboard. Use only .jpg files for photos as this format handles far more colors than .gif, which only displays a max of 256 colors. Use .gifs for images with only a few colors like black and whites. The most popular Facebook profiles have a uniform theme throughout and your photo(s) are one of the best ways to quickly show your profile's theme and your interests.

BLACK AND WHITE PHOTOS ARE COOL

Black and white photos are all the rage on Facebook. If you want to add a coolness factor to your photos make them black and white and use .gif format. These work especially well with a dark profile background like black or gray. If you are going for the gothic look or have a cutting edge band, a B&W photo is a must.

Remember that Facebook has the right to review and remove any photo at any time. They do not even have to give a reason. Since very hi-res, large photos must be shrunk down to fit Facebook's 4MB file size limitation; use a free graphics program to do it.

One remedy to the hi-res issue is to switch your digital camera to low-res mode. For size issues you can simply use Microsoft Paint that comes with free with all PCs.

Resize Photos in Microsoft Paint Table 5.F
➢ Click on Start Button → Select All Programs → Accessories
➢ Load Paint → Open your .gif or .jpg photo/image
➢ Shrink selected photo/image → Resave to new file name
➢ Upload resaved file to Facebook

UNLIMITED PHOTO UPLOADS

With Facebook, you can upload unlimited photos to your profile. Image hosting sites such as PhotoBucket.com or Flickr.com or ImageShack.com let you upload unlimited photos and that is a main reason why they are so popular.

For other resize options, you can get a free copy of IrfanView. Use it to resize images so they're 4MB or less in size, or resave images that may be corrupted. Table 5.G shows you how.

Resize Photos in IrfanView Table 5.G
➢ Download IrfanView from www.irfanview.com
➢ Run IrfanView from your computer → Open your .gif, or .jpg photo/image
➢ Resize photo/image → Resave photo/image to new file name
➢ Upload resaved file to Facebook

RIGHT CLICK TO ADD ANY PHOTO AS WALLPAPER

Any photo on Facebook that has not been privacy protected can be right clicked on and emailed (select "Email Picture"), or set as your PC background photo or wallpaper, by selecting "Set as Background". As always, make sure no one owns a copyright in the photo.

Some Facebookers do not realize you can easily adjust the thumbnail of your default photo that is shown when you post on The Wall and in search results. To access this feature click Edit → Picture → under Thumbnail Version drag the image to adjust →

click Save Thumbnail Version. This is needed because the thumbnail is a square picture and most uploads are a vertical rectangles.

C. Making a Photo Standout on Friends' Profiles

If you happen to be the friend of a very popular person, it's difficult to make your profile standout when it's competing with so many others. Many people don't realize it, but the size of your photo can make you stand above the rest. Take the following case study into consideration of a very popular person who attends Mississippi State. Here, the typical 6 friends are shown in this Facebooker's friend space in the Mississippi State network. See how Kristen's photo towers above the rest. Why? She uploaded a vertical photo and the others did not! This is huge to getting recognized on Facebook.

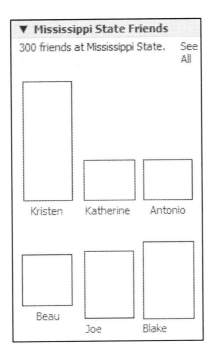

And while Facebook crops photos to make thumbnails out of them, they are not cropped when shown on profiles. So get out there and use as your default photo a vertical photo shot from your digital camera, keeping in mind that it cannot be over 4MB in size.

D. Create a New Photo Album

Like everything with Facebook, creating a new photo album is simple. Click on Photos → select Create a Photo Album.

Let's say you want to create an entirely new photo album of your trip to Bermuda. No problem. Facebook gives you 65 total characters to name the album, including spaces. You have unlimited characters to describe the location and likewise for the description. Click on any existing album name and you are presented with a screen that lets you change the name. Easy enough.

NO HTML - SYMBOLS OK

You cannot use HTML in photo album titles, locations or descriptions, but you can copy and paste symbols from a word processing program such as Microsoft Word into these sections. So make your albums stand out.

Be sure to visit the privacy chapter of *Facebook Fanatic* and review the privacy settings for photos. Here are your options for album privacy that you select when creating a new album.

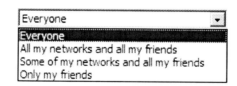

Click any album name and you will be presented with the option to delete it. Once you delete an album you cannot restore it absent uploading *all* photos again, which is a very daunting task for most of us.

E. Photo Widgets

What on earth is a widget? Think of them as mini applications loaded onto your Facebook profile that enable you to show the world cool things . . . like a photo slideshow right on your profile or glitter text or a ranking of your hottest friends. Where are you going to find these widgets? Don't worry. You do not have to embark on a wild

Internet search for Facebook widgets or search Nottingham Forest. The Facebook Development Platform enables the Web's top coders to create widget applications that work seamlessly with Facebook. To find the widgets click on developers at the bottom of any page or conduct a search for "photo applications".

You will then be presented with a number of categories in the left-hand column. Select Product Directory to view an extensive list of applications that are available.

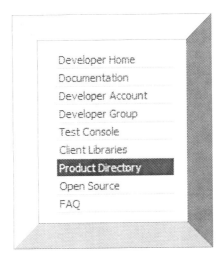

Here are some of our favorite photo widgets. The first is called A Thousand Words and with it you can make a photographic representation of Facebook and your friends. Visit http://students.washington.edu/myonmine/a1000word/index.php to get the application.

A Thousand Words

Your Hottest Friend enables you to set up voting for your hottest friend photos. Not only is this tons of fun, but it can sure put friends in their place who aren't as good looking as they think they are! Find this app at: yourhottestfriend.com.

Your Hottest Friend

Rock You Slideshows are a great way to allow for photo slideshows of your Facebook photos. Rock You is also popular on other social networking sites like Bebo.com. Get this app at: rockyou.com.

RockYou

Do you have tons of cool photos in your Mac but don't want to take the time to upload each of them individually to Facebook? If yes, the iPhoto Facebook exporter allows you to export photos from iPhoto directly into your profile.

iPhoto Exporter

This is a huge time saver. You must, however, have Mac OS X 10.4 or later for it to work. Follow this link to get it: http://developers.facebook.com/iphoto/.

UPLOAD ENTIRE FOLDER
It's faster to upload an entire folder or album from iPhoto and delete the photos you don't want once they are on Facebook than to pick and choose.

FBTF stands for Facebook To Flickr and it allows you to export photos from Facebook to your Flickr account. Not only is this a time saver, but it allows you to show family members your Facebook photos who may not have access to Facebook because of your privacy settings or because they simply aren't on Facebook (like Granny Mary). You can get this handy application at: telcobox.net/FBTF/index.php. There are so many photo widgets it's hard to pick! But for photos, slideshow widgets are all the rage.

FBTF

F. Distributing a Facebook Photo

Facebook is a fantastic place to meet friends and to show great photos about who you are and what you're about. If you want to share these photos with friends outside of the Facebook network, here are some great ways to do it apart from the normal send photo designation within Facebook. First, however, you have to learn your Facebook photo URL.

Steps to Learn a Facebook Photo URL
Table 5.H
➢ Click on Any Photo in Facebook → Once photo is enlarged, right click on it
➢ Select Properties from dropdown → Highlight URL field (.jpg or .gif ending)
➢ Right click on highlighted URL field and select copy

1. Add Facebook Photo to AIM Box

Once you have copied a photo's URL as laid out above, you must now paste it into HTML code that will automatically link to the photo on Facebook. AOL Instant Messenger allows you to attach information to your screen name so that people can read it even when you are not online. This is your AIM calling card. You can easily provide a hyperlink to your Facebook profile and show your default photo.

Steps to Show Your Facebook Photo Via AIM Info Box Table 5.I
➢ Log into AIM and select My AIM →Edit Profile ➢ Click on Next until you reach the More Info screen ➢ Paste this HTML code into the window: <a href="http://[YOUR FACEBOOK URL] target="_blank"><img src=[COPIED URL] border="0" alt="" /> <img src="" border="0" alt="" /> <font size="1" face="Veranda, Arial, Helvetica, sans-serif">Visit my Facebook profile!</font></a> → Click on Finish and you are all set

2. Add Facebook Photo to Yahoo Mail Signature

Yahoo allows you to attach photos to your Yahoo Mail signature block. Here is how to do it with an easy Facebook HTML tag.

Steps to Show Your Facebook Photo on Yahoo Mail Signatures Table 5.J
➢ Sign into your Yahoo Mail account ➢ Select Mail Options → Signature → Color and Graphics link ➢ Check *both* the Add Signature and View HTML Source boxes ➢ Paste this HTML code into the window: <a href="http://[YOUR FACEBOOK URL] target="_blank"><img src=[COPIED URL] border="0" alt="" /> <img src="" border="0" alt="" /> <font size="1" face="Veranda, Arial, Helvetica, sans-serif">Check me out on Facebook!</font></a> ➢ Click on Save at the bottom of the profile and you are all set

3. Add Facebook Photo to a Website

If you have a Website, it is easy to add a URL link and your Facebook default photo. Then, if visitors to your site want to check out what you have cookin' on Facebook, all they have to do is click. Here are the steps:

Steps to Show Facebook Photo on Your Website
Table 5.K
➢ Open your Website in your HTML authoring software such as Microsoft FrontPage ➢ In Design view, position your cursor where you want the link inserted ➢ Click the Code tab at the bottom on the screen ➢ Paste this HTML code where your cursor is blinking: <a href="http://[YOUR FACEBOOK URL] target="_blank"><img src=[COPIED URL] border="0" alt="" />
<img src="" border="0" alt="" />
<font size="1" face="Veranda, Arial, Helvetica, sans-serif">Visit my Facebook profile!</font></a> ➢ Save modified profile → Upload Web profile to your Website's host server

I. Profile Views and Last Active

The number and quality of the photos you upload to Facebook is key to the number of profile views you will receive. Unfortunately, page views and profile views are not shown on your profile. Last Active is the last time you logged in to Facebook. Unlike most other social networking sites, Facebook does not display the last time you logged in even on News Feed or Mini-Feed.

J. Deleting Profile Photo

Tired of your default photo? Well you can replace it by uploading a new one or simply delete it. To remove your default photo click Edit → Picture tab → select "Remove Picture" from the bottom of the page. Note that if you don't replace the picture, you will have the dreaded question mark shown in its place until you do. And this is a tough way to make new friends.

60 Second Summary

Key Photo Tips
• Photo size limited to 4MB • Allowed photo file types are .jpg, .gif, and .png • Rotate profile photo often to keep profile fresh • Facebook allows unlimited photo uploads • Easily send Facebook photos by email

What You'll Experience

Change Top Friends

How to Get, Keep & Delete Friends

NewsFeed & Mini-Feed

Climbing The Wall

VI   Friend Space

A. Friends – How to Get, Keep and Delete Them

On Facebook, friends are like money—you just can't have enough. And we've learned that your photo is key to attracting many of them. We also learned in the privacy chapter that certain information can be shielded from even direct friends. For the next couple of pages we'll explore how to find new and old friends on Facebook since your friend space is the heart of your popularity engine. Your friends' space is the holding area for all your friends; well . . . their photos anyway. You can delete them, poke them, message them, and even take a look at upcoming birthdays.

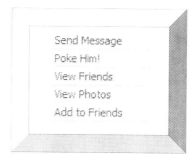

1. Adding Friends

Adding new friends is fundamental to your existence on Facebook. No friends = no fun. The three ways you can contact potential new friends on Facebook are by sending a friend request, shooting a message or poking them. To do any of this, you first have to find friends on Facebook. Click on Friends → Find Friends.

| Friend List | Find Friends | Status Updates | Social Timeline |

Fortunately, it's easy to locate friends on Facebook that are your existing friends outside of Facebook. Some may already be on Facebook and you have no clue. As you can imagine, Facebook has been very successful at adding new users by email invites since there are so many of them. You can also find current and former high school and college friends already on Facebook, as well as coworkers. Once a friend is located, just click on the Add to Friends link. This will send an invite to them from you. If they accept, they will appear in your friends' list.

a. Friends Already on Facebook

When you click on Friends at the top of the screen, you are taken to a screen that displays your friends' photos. Fine. Below that you are asked to locate other existing friends in Facebook that may already be registered. How is this accomplished? Facebook lets you send out a message to those in your email address books on AOL, Gmail, Hotmail, Hotmail.co.uk, Hotmail.ca, MSN and Yahoo.com, Yahoo.ca, and Yahoo.co.uk. The default is your Facebook sign-in email program.

gmail.com
hotmail.com
yahoo.com
gmail.com
aol.com
msn.com
hotmail.co.uk
yahoo.co.uk
yahoo.ca
hotmail.ca
msn.ca
other...

Once you give Facebook your email address and password, its computer algorithms automatically gather your email address book contacts. The list of those on Facebook will appear and you select which to contact. The default is that *all* names are checked so clicking "Invite to Join" will send an invite to everyone on Facebook you have ever emailed on your email program.

> **Invite to Join**   **Skip and Go Home**

You can even invite people to join Facebook who you have emailed, but are not on Facebook. You will be presented with the entire list once you have left the area for those already on Facebook. Once again the default is that all email addresses will be checked to

> Search every 6 months for new friends that have joined Facebook.

send a Facebook invite. Be sure to delete any friends or relatives from the list that you do not want to receive the invite. Be aware that when you contact friends in your email address books your photo will be attached to your email message.

GET A QUICK LIST OF EMAIL ADDRESSES
Want to get a quick list of all your email clients? Just click and highlight from the list Facebook presents. You will have to do a bit of editing in a word processor afterwards.

b. High School Friends
Many high schools are quite large. It's not unusual to have hundreds of students in a class. With many students it's likely a few of your high school friends are on Facebook but you don't know it. If they have signed up as attending your high school (and so have you) they will be searchable within this network as well as your region network. But there is a quicker way to find them than combing through search results. You can simply search for them by clicking on Friends → Friend List → select "Find former high school classmates" and you are shown a form where you pick the school, city and name.

c. College Friends
Want to rekindle a romance with a former college flame or get in touch with an old sorority classmate? No problem. Facebook makes it easy. If they have signed up as attending your college (and so have you) they will be searchable within this network. But there is a quicker way to find them than combing through search results. You can simply search for them by clicking on Friends → Friend List → select "Find current or

past college classmates" and you will be presented with a form where you search on college, class year and name.

NAME MAY NOT BE THE SAME

Keep in mind that your old college friends may have gotten married and changed their name or are just using the first letter of their last name. If this is the case the name field may be of little use.

d. Coworkers

With Facebook's you can even locate former and current coworkers on the site. This can come in especially handy when trying to find that guy who always used to make you laugh when standing around the water cooler. Search for them by clicking on Friends → Friend List → select "Find current or past coworkers" and you can search on company and employee name.

> Facebook has no control over email sent from clients outside of the site such as Gmail. If you get spam from outside the network it is not Facebook's fault.

e. Adding Friends Within Facebook

If you run across a cool profile of a Facebooker who you have tons in common with, send them a message and ask to become their friend. Just click Send Message.

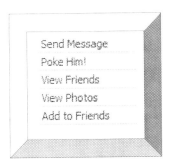

They will check out your profile and if they like what they read and see, then they can ask to add you as a friend and all you have to do is accept. A more direct way to add friends within Facebook is to click on Add to Friends. You then verify you want to add this person. Since getting a new friend is a two-way street, Facebook will message them with the request. They can accept or deny your request to add them as a friend.

1000 MESSAGES IS THE LIMIT

In the wake of the tragic shootings in Virginia, some schools and colleges have set up a designated individual to blast emergency messages to students on Facebook. At present, Facebook limits messages sent out to 1000 individuals, but this may change in the near future.

2. Friends Shown on Profile

Once you have a bunch of friends on Facebook you may want to change their positions around. Friends are added and shown chronologically in your friend space. Friends added first appear at the top of your space. On Facebook only 6 friend photos are shown on the front page of your profile. That is why it is so important to get added as one of the first friends of a

Facebookers visiting your profile can view all your friends by clicking on View All in the lower right-hand corner of your friend space.

popular person, band or politician. If you are one of the 6 friends your photo will be seen when others visit the profile and this greatly increases the chance they will click on your photo. If you have *more* than 6 friends, Facebook will randomly rotate them on your profile. That is why it's so important to be in the first 6 since you are guaranteed a spot on your friend's profile until they get more than 6 friends. For some this could take months or years. When a friend changes their default photo, it will change across the entire Facebook network. That means the new photo will appear on your profile and in any comments they have left on The Wall.

3. Delete Friends

Let's say you signed up for Facebook six months ago, when you had an old boyfriend and he was the first friend you added. His photo is displayed first in your friends' space. This can obviously get Embarrassing, especially when your new boyfriend pokes around your profile. Do not fear. Just delete your old boyfriend as a friend. This will immediately stop him from being able to post comments to your profile. It's fun to delete old flames, but even better to add new ones!

WANT TO DISAPPEAR?

If you zap a friend from your friend space, do not worry. They will not be notified and all your contact information will be automatically erased along with your photo from their friend list.

B. News Feed and Mini-Feed for Friend Updates

If you build a large group of friends using the Facebook tips and tricks in this book, which is likely, it will be hard to keep track of them all. Your friend space will be huge and you may not have enough time to monitor all the comments and Wall stuff they are posting on your profile. Friend updates are a way to keep track of what your close friends are doing on your Facebook profile. On Facebook these tracking applications are called News Feed and Mini-Feed. They were controversial when first launched. Facebook quickly added privacy features that calmed most people's concerns.

If you are not familiar with these two applications, News Feed updates what profile changes you have made and announces them on your friends' profiles and likewise their changes are displayed on your profile. Mini-Feed shows updates you've made on your own profile for those who may be visiting.

> The maximum number of Mini-Feeds shown on your profile at any one time is 10. This cannot be changed.

▼ Mini-Feed

Displaying 1 story..   See All

Not only that, but with Mini-Feed a person can click on "See All" to see *every* change you have ever made on your profile! This can raise privacy issues for some. News Feed also includes activity happening in social groups such as networks and groups to which you belong. At first it is confusing as to what is published on News Feed and Mini-Feed and what is not. So here is a breakdown.

Things that May be Published on News Feed & Mini-Feed	Things Never Published on News Feed & Mini-Feed
➤ Additions to Profile	➤ Events You Decline
➤ Content Posted to Profile	➤ Friend Requests You Reject
➤ Events Attended or Created	➤ Friends You Remove
➤ Groups Joined or Created	➤ Groups You Decline to Join
➤ Networks Joined	➤ Messages Sent
➤ Notes Written	➤ Notes Deleted
➤ Notes You're Tagged in	➤ Notes Read – by Whom
➤ Photos You're Tagged in	➤ Photos Deleted
➤ Photos Uploaded	➤ Photos Viewed – by Whom
➤ Status Updates	➤ Pokies & Whose Profiles Viewed

1. Publish Stories When I . . .

If you want to prevent Facebook from publishing a newsflash when you do any of the things below, just uncheck the appropriate boxes. As a default, all boxes are checked.

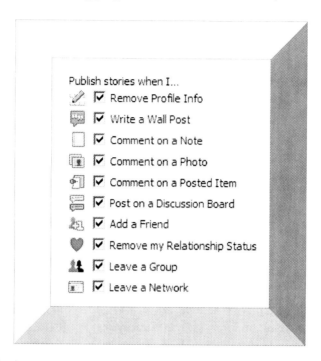

2. Show Times of Stories

News Feed and Mini-Feed automatically post the times of your profile changes and this is the default setting. To turn it off just uncheck the box below and remember to click on Save Changes before returning to your profile.

TURN OFF TIMES IF USING AT WORK OR SCHOOL

If you are brave enough to use Facebook at work or school, do not show the times in News Feed or Mini-Feed or risk losing your job when a co-worker visits your profile.

3. View Birthdays

Facebook makes it easy to see when it is your friend's birthday. When you sign-in to Facebook you will be presented with fiends' upcoming birthdays. They are automatically displayed on your profile. Simply click on the "See All" link and any birthday of your friends in the next month will be shown.

Birthdays   see all

No upcoming birthdays.

Good practice is to click on this link the 1st of every month to ensure you see all the birthdays coming up and can shoot off an instant message or send your gift on time. Of course this will not be an issue if you send a digital gift on Facebook. More about digital gifts later.

MONTH AND DATE USUALLY RIGHT

You can change your age on Facebook at anytime within the edit profile section of your account profile, but the majority of people list the real month and day of their birth even if the year is fudged.

4. Facebookers with the Most Friends

Getting friends on Facebook builds upon itself. You start off with a few close friends then friends of theirs want you as a friend and so and so on, until you have hundreds of friends. Building a huge stack of friends on Facebook is the best legal pyramid scheme you will find. So, who is the most popular on Facebook? Who has the most friends? According to The Book War (thebookwar.com), a Facebook Developer Application, Hayley W. of Ohio State does with a whopping 1216 friends. Visit http://osu.facebook.com/s.php?k=10080&id=12453669 to see all her friends. Ms Porsche Dee K. of MTSU has 1075 friends. Her Member ID is 38411277. Dave M. who is only on the Facebook network, has1066 friends and a Member ID of 10200882. Mishal H. of Tallahassee, Florida has 1013 friends and a Member ID of 503396231. Rounding out our Top 5 is Rachelle E. of Carnegie Mellon with 867 friends and a Member ID of 4800181. There are likely others on Facebook with more friends, but who have not enabled The Book War application.

In your quest to get the most friends, remember that Facebook requires visitors to contact you first to see if they can be your friend. Be sure to do your due diligence by checking out the Facebook profile of the requestor to see if they would make a good friend just like you do in the real world. With friends on Facebook, the sky is the limit. Some of the most popular people on Facebook have literally hundreds of friends and you must scroll down page after page to view them after clicking "See All".

C. Keep Friends Updated on Your Status

Friends want to know what you are doing when not poking them on Facebook. And if they are your good friends, they will excuse you for not being on Facebook 24/7/365. Status Updates are a quick way to let the Facebook world know when you are unavailable. Select Friends → Status Updates.

Plus, Status Updates are a way to stop annoying IMs and cellphone calls by friends asking where you are. Status Updates are also published on News Feed and Mini-Feeds. Here is a list of the Status Update categories. Yes, you are allowed to sleep instead of being on Facebook.

One of the best ways to keep friends informed is by enabling Status Updates on your mobile device. Under the various categories, on the right-hand side of the screen you will see the Mobile Status Updates icon.

With Mobile Status Updates you can send and get friend updates from mobile devices worldwide. Your cellular provider may, however, charge a fee for sending and receiving Mobile Status Updates depending upon your payment plan. It's also important to note that you must sign up for Friends' Status Updates. Likewise, they must do the same to receive your Status Updates.

If you have a lot of friends and their Status Updates are quickly becoming the new spam in your life, you can disable them at any time.

D. Social Timelines

We are all familiar with timelines from history class or project deadlines at work. Facebook has its own version. Just click Friends → Social Timeline.

To best understand Social Timelines on Facebook, think of a timeline for your life. On the left side is the date of your birth, when you started to walk, the first day of Kindergarten, the first time you rode a two-wheel bike, etc. Now for a Social Timeline, you can track when you first met your friends, when your sports team won the championship, your first kiss, etc. You get the picture. Best of all, you can include as many friends as you want on the Social Timeline. To get started, click over to your Friend List by selecting Friends → Friend List and then click "How do you know . . ." for each of them. Follow the easy instructions and walk through the steps presented. It's simple to create and fun to see a graphical timeline of your life in the social setting.

E. Post on Public Profiles

Getting popular on Facebook can increase by a simple act that will get you noticed and tons of clicks to your profile. Here's the secret. Listen carefully. Post on The Wall of public profiles like events and Facebook Diaries. You can even post video comments!

Befriend the hottest profiles on Facebook today and be sure to post comments to get clicks over to your profile. If the profile is in check with the theme of your profile, all the better. That means visitors to the profile will be more likely to find your profile interesting and want to become your friend. And friends = popularity on Facebook.

KEEP PROFILE FRESH

Click in the top bar of any profile section (except) Newsfeed and Mini-Feed to move a section up, down, left or right in your profile. Keep it fresh. This includes changing your photo every so often as discussed.

Tip

F. Befriend a Celebrity

There is an old proverb that says they who want friends must make themselves friendly, or something like that. The same applies to Facebook. Stop hiding within the confines of your profile and get out there and *make* new friends. A great place to start is with movie stars. Most of the mega stars (Brad Pitt, Tom Cruise, Angelina Jolie, etc.) do not have Facebook profiles, yet a number of up and coming stars do have profiles to get their names out there and to establish a fan base.

AUTOMATIC CELEBRITY ADDS

Like many areas of their lives, celebrities have "their people" accept friend requests on Facebook. This "accept pretty much anyone who sends me a friend request" is your ticket to getting a celebrity as your friend.

Tip

It may seem that a person who is on a hit TV show would never want to be your friend, but the reality is just the opposite. Think about it. A huge fan base is the lifeblood of a celebrity. They need you just as much or more than you need them. Do not forget about non-movie/TV celebrities like

If you get a famous friend, post a "Thanks for the Add" comment to get even more exposure on their popular profile.

sports stars (for some reason there is a lot of big-time wrestling stars on Facebook), authors, and comedians.

G. Give a Digital Gift

Sending a gift is a great way to show friends that you care about them. You can send a balloon or cake on a birthday or a karate chop. The possibilities are endless. What's great is that each icon can have so many different meanings. Your first gift is free and after that they cost $1 each. There are over 150 gifts

You can only get digital gifts from direct friends. Likewise you can only give gifts to direct friends.

to give with more being added all the time. Popular ones expire so dish them out quickly.

You can also add a message that will be included along with your gift. It is up to you whether the message will be publicly viewable. When a friend receives a gift, it will be displayed on their profile. There are 3 privacy settings for gifts: Public, Private and Anonymous and here is their breakdown.

Privacy Setting	Gift Shown?	Message Shown?	Name Shown?
Public	Yes – Gift Box & Wall	Yes	Yes
Private	Yes – Gift Box Only	No	Not Publicly
Anonymous	Yes – Gift Box Only	No	No

Spending a dollar is an inexpensive way to impress a good friend and can be even more personal that a real gift given all the icons you can select from on Facebook.

H. Create a Facebook Badge

Do you want to let the world know about your cool profile outside of Facebook? Do you have a Website that you would like to include a graphic on that links to your Facebook profile? How about a Note outside of Facebook? Got a MySpace page you want to link to Facebook? If so, Facebook has the easy answer. It's called Facebook Badges and with them you can provide a splashy graphic that lets the world click over to your Facebook profile. You have total control on what info you place in them. Got your own personal Website apart from Facebook? If so, this is a great place for your Badge. Let's get started by clicking on Profile → Create a Profile Badge beneath your photo.

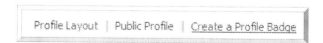

You have a wide selection of items to include in your Badges, but remember to never information in your Badge than you have divulged on your profile.

Facebook Badge Items Table 6.A
➤ Birthday; Email; Latest Notes; Mobile Number; Name; Networks; Posts
➤ Recent Pics by Me; Screen Name; Status Updates; Upcoming Events
➤ Websites

1. Designing Your Own Badge

Facebook gives you four options when creating a Badge and the first is a custom Badge that comes preset with your profile picture, name and networks to which you belong.

The default layout is horizontal and the format created for the Badge is an image. Just click Add Item when finished and Facebook will create the Badge and give you HTML code to insert into your Website. Here is an example with the profile picture, Facebook name, and networks included.

You have unlimited items to place within your Facebook Badge so use them to your heart's content.

<a href="http://www.facebook.com/p/Andy_B/527300036" title="Andy B's Facebook profile" target=_TOP><img src="http://badge.facebook.com/badge/527300036.874.1448866003.png" border=0 alt="Andy B's Facebook profile"></a>

As you can see, the title of this Badge will be "Andy B's Facebook profile" and a link is provided to his Facebook profile. Here is an example.

2. Preset Note Badge

If you don't want to work to create your own Badge, Facebook has three preset Badges for your pleasure. The Note Badge is unique in that it is the only preset Badge where the layout is oriented in the vertical direction as most Notes extend down the page in vertical fashion. The four default items are these and you can add or subtract from them at will.

What is also unique with the Note Badge is that script is the default image format since most all Notes are written in script. Here is an example.

3. Photo Badge

The preset Photo Badge is a good way to get your photos out on the Internet and get people clicking over to your profile on Facebook. In fact, it is not your default profile photo that is the default item, but rather your recent photos stored in your photo albums. The default layout is horizontal and the format created for the Badge is an image. Add other items as you see fit.

4. Signature Badge

The Signature Badge is the present Badge that gives away the most personal information about yourself, including your email address. Remember, Facebook will not display your email address on your profile if you don't want it to, but that does not stop it from being placed in a Badge unless you change the email item.

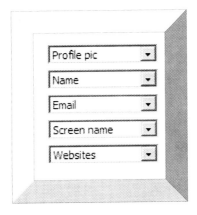

For the Signature Badge the default layout is horizontal and the format created for the Badge is an image.

<u>COME ON OVER FROM MYSPACE</u>
If you also have a MySpace profile and like Facebook better, inserting your Facebook Badge HTML code into any MySpace interest section will display the badge and direct your MySpace friends over to Facebook.

60 Second Summary

Key Friend Space Tips

- Use signatures to invite friends to join Facebook who are in your Hotmail, Gmail, AOL and Yahoo Mail address books
- Your friends' photos are shown on your profile and rotated
- Search for new friends on Facebook on a periodic basis
- Facebook Badges are a good way to get profile traffic from Websites
- Give digital gifts to impress friends

What You'll Experience

Share YouTube Videos

Get a Digital Pet

Demand a Band

Be a Loan Shark

Slideshow Photos

VII   Top Facebook Apps

A. Apps Introduction

Facebook started out as a closed social networking system. The only allowed applications were those created by Facebook developers. This all changed in 2007 when Facebook announced that it was opening its digital robe to enable any developer to create applications that add functionality to Facebook profiles. Since that time over a thousand applications have been developed and there are more on the way. This book would be remiss without showing you some of the hottest Facebook apps so you can add them to your profile. Major application developers, which have previously been coding for Bebo and MySpace, have gotten involved. *The Wall Street Journal* reported that the Facebook app "Where I've Been" that shows graphically the places where a person has visited, was sold for $3 million to Expedia. Talk about lunch money! Other sites like RockYou.com enable you to use its GlitterText, and PhotoFX to add a splash to your photos. It also has a feature to countdown future events. SnapVine.com allows you to add voice recording functionality to your profile so that friends can leave you a voice message. Play it back the next time you login. There are so many new apps it's hard to pick! Here are some of the best.

B. Get a Digital Pet

One of the hottest Facebook apps has nothing to do with videos or photos or other traditional media. The app is the Pets application and with it you can pick a digital pet and arm them to battle other pets. How cool!

Get the app by visiting http://www.facebook.com/apps/application.php?id=2419681379. Your pet can fight to its heart's content, but be sure, however, to feed it. Friends can also join in the act and help feed your digital pet. Trick out your pet today by adding amour! Best of all, there is no mess to clean up and they will never eat your homework.

C. Be a Digital Loan Shark

If you are in need of cash, the Lending Club lets you borrow money from the Facebook community at set rates the lenders are willing to offer. If you want to be a lender, this application is a great way for you to get a high return on your money.

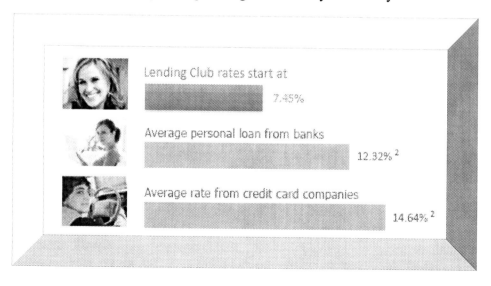

Find the app at: http://utulsa.facebook.com/apps/application.php?id=2360494761. Once you sign up, you are on your way to getting cash without hidden fees or by dealing with a bank or credit card company. At the moment it is only available in the United States and Canada.

WATCH YOUR CREDIT SCORE

At present, Facebook requires that you use your real name. You do not, however, have to include your full last name. The first letter of your last name will suffice and you can put your nickname between your first and last names. As a borrower, you must have a FICO score of at least 640 to get money. To check your credit score first, go to FreeCreditReport.com or any other free credit score service.

D. Show Off Groups

If you have the right privacy settings disabled, you can show off what groups you belong to on Facebook and you can belong to a maximum of 200 groups. What is lacking is that photos for the groups are not shown and you cannot reorder them if you belong to tons of groups. Now there is a way to spice your groups and show them off at the same time. It's called Top Groups.

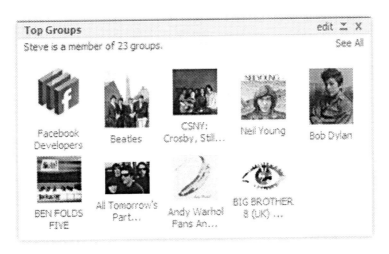

Find this app at: http://www.facebook.com/apps/application.php?id=2601931318.
With this handy application you can show photos

SECRET GROUPS ARE SHOWN

The bottom line with the Top Groups app is that if you don't want to have your secret groups revealed, do not place them within the Top Groups app.

E. Demand Your Band

Live in a small town and never get the cool bands? Do you want to cry out for your favorite to visit a city nearby so you can go see them? Are you the biggest fan of an indie band and can get hundreds of friends out to support them in a live show? If the answer is yes to any of these questions, then the Demands application is for you.

This app is unlimited. You can include comedians, politicians, etc.

Find this app at: http://utulsa.facebook.com/apps/application.php?id=2471711738. Eventful, the creator, states that over 10,000 bands, comedians and politicians are using the app to route their tours. Get with your friends and make your voices heard!

F. Endorse and Elect

If you are politically motivated, you can now show your true colors on Facebook by endorsing candidates right on your profile with the Election app. This is a very powerful tool if you are popular on Facebook as you can influence tons of people with your political views. You can get started by pointing your Internet browser to: http://apps.facebook.com/apps/application.php?id=2360172394&b and let your political feelings be known in a not so subtle way.

G. Rock Your Photos

Okay, like everybody else on Facebook you have a few photos on your profile and Facebookers can see them with a little work by accessing your photo albums. If you want to bring your photos to life and have an uber cool profile, then the SlideShow application by RockYou is a must.

SLIDESHOWS & PHOTOS
BY ROCKYOU

Visit http://www.facebook.com/apps/application.php?id=2343264586&b to get the app and launch your photos into the popularity stratosphere today.

H. Show Videos with myTV

We all know that YouTube is the current leader in Internet video. Yeah, most of it is grainy, but the inventory is there for nearly any category under the digital sun. The Facebook video player does not let you show YouTube videos directly and that creates a problem for some. Never fear. To skirt this conundrum get the myTV application.

Find this app here so can begin showing YouTube videos on your profile today: http://www.facebook.com/apps/application.php?api_key=7c1cdf5087d34bf3bcf72f05a7d49545. What's more, you can search for top YouTube videos right from your profile. You can also import your favorites list right from YouTube. This powerful tool is free!

With myTV create your own video playlists and place *unlimited* videos in them to show on your profile.

I. Have a Food Fight

The Food Fight application is being splattered all across Facebook. From eggplant to pickles to nachos to ice cream, you can throw digital food at your friends and enemies on Facebook. You start with free "lunch money" each day and must pay for each item of food you through ranging from $10 for lobster to $.25 for watermelon (when it's in season)! When the money is spent for the day, you must wait for the next day to get more food money just like in real life. Search for "Food Fight Application" and get the app today.

J. Show Your College's Shield

In the UK colleges have unique shields that show off their school's true colors. If you attend(ed) Oxford, Cambridge or Durham Colleges and want to show yours off on your profile, follow these links:

Facebook College Shields Table 7.A
Cambridge: http://www.facebook.com/apps/application.php?id=2389312388&ref=s
Durham: http://www.facebook.com/apps/application.php?id=2505610204&ref=s
Oxford: http://www.facebook.com/apps/application.php?id=2392939361&ref=s

Oxford College has its official Facebook student group. You can find it here: http://oxford.facebook.com/group.php?   While we're talking about colleges, here is a great site called Campus Grotto that displays college applications that will make you more productive at college. And who doesn't need that?

campusgrotto.com/best-facebook-applications-for-college.html

60 Second Summary

Key Facebook Apps

- Raise a digital pet with the Pets app
- The Top Groups app lets you show photos of all your groups on your profile
- Be a digital loan shark with Lending Club
- Request a band to visit your town with the Demands app
- Endorse a candidate on your profile with the Elections app
- Rock your photos with the SlideShow app
- The myTV app lets you show any YouTube videos right on your profile
- Get the Food Fight application and splatter friends and enemies

What You'll Experience

Create a Facebook Flyer

Reporting Events

Global Events on Facebook

Event Attire

VIII   Events & Flyers

A. Facebook Events

Feeling lonely? Not if you are on Facebook. It's your one stop shop for learning where the coolest parties are, art exhibits, and sporting events. Think of Facebook Events as a calendar on steroids where you can learn about events and the people who are organizing them within your networks. With Facebook Events the possibilities to be seen with the hippest people and stay in touch with friends are endless.

 **Events**

To get started with Facebook Events, and to know what all your groovy friends are planning, just click the events link on the left-hand side of your profile. Then you will be presented with your upcoming events. At the top of the screen you can browse for events, create one and even export them. We'll explore each in detail, starting with how to browse for events in the most effective manner.

There are eight types of events: Causes (think activism), Education, Meetings, Music/Arts, Other (the world is your oyster), Party, Sports, and Trips. We will discuss the subcategories for each in the Creating an Event section.

1. Browsing Events

It's fun to peruse through events happening in your networks where you can quickly learn where the event is being held, who is the host, and when it is happening. Just click on Browse Events at the top of your screen to be taken to page-after-page of events.

Events you can attend will have an Add to My Events link in the upper right-hand corner. Clicking on these links will add the event to your calendar.

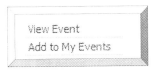

You, of course, will not be obligated to attend, but at least it will be on your schedule. For privacy concerns, realize that the host of the event will also be able to see that you have signed up.

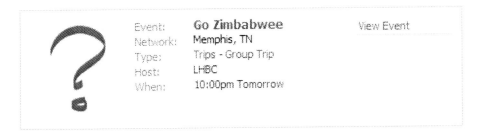

CHECK OUT THE GLOBAL NETWORK

Click the arrow under Network and you can pick the Other network, which is the Global network. This is great to use when traveling to find the coolest parties, concerts and art exhibits while on the road.

You can always search directly for events by inputting a search query in the Search for Events box on the events homepage.

Search for Events

One of the best ways to do it is to input your school's name, or whatever network you are part of, to get a list of all the events happening in the near future. Winnow it down from there. The date options for search that you have are: Today, Tomorrow, One Week, or One Month. Once you find an event of interest, just click View Event and you will be taken to the event's profile. There you will learn detailed information about the event like directions, contact telephone number, and whether guests can bring friends to the event.

How to Report an Event on Facebook Table 8.A
➢ Login → Click on events → Browse or search for event
➢ Select View Event → Under event photo Click on Report Event

On each event page you will be able to see what friends have accepted the invitation (Confirmed Guests), who cannot attend, those who maybe attending, and those that have not replied. Six Confirmed Guest photos are displayed on the profile at any one time. Just like friends on a normal profile, Facebook rotates them. Only three photos are displayed for those maybe attending, not attending, and that have yet to reply.

CAN'T MAKE IT – POST ON THE WALL

A great way for you to draw attention to your profile and stay in the good graces of invitees is to post on The Wall a "Sorry I cannot make it" statement or short video.

2. Creating an Event

Creating an event on Facebook can be almost as fun as the event itself. Click on Create an Event and begin the three-step process where you input event info, photo and the guest list.

Browse Events   Create an Event   Export Events

Here are key Facebook event tips that will make your outing a success before it even beings. Preparation for a great event begins on Facebook!

a. Title

The title is the first written introduction to your event. Make sure it is on point and does not ramble. You have plenty of space in the description section to disclose why your event is cool. Try to limit your title to five words or less. Facebook gives you 75 characters in which to title your event, including spaces. Within reason, your event name can be anything you want. Facebook does not, however, allow you to place HTML in an event's name.

b. Taglines

Your tagline is very important to your event's success. Have a dull tagline and people won't feel the need to attend, while a splashy tagline can make your event a hit. Use call to action words like "last chance", "get it while it's hot", "be there or be square", "rock the house", "we're rockin' the house", etc. Use plenty of verbs and save the basics for the title. Buzz your event before it starts. You have unlimited characters for your tagline so don't be shy.

c. Categories and Types

There are eight different event categories on Facebook. Within each are numerous types or subcategories. Here's a listing for each. And, of course, party has the most subcategories!

Event Categories & Types Table 8.B

Party
  ➤ Bar Night; Barbecue; Benefit; Birthday Party; Card Night; Cocktail Party
  ➤ Club Party; Dinner Party; Drinking Games; Erotic Party
  ➤ Fraternity/Sorority Party; Goodbye Party; Holiday Party; House Party
  ➤ LAN Party; Mixer; Movie/TV Night; Night of Mayhem; Reunion
  ➤ Slumber Party

Causes   ➤ Fundraiser; Rally; Protest
Education   ➤ Class; Lecture; Office Hours; Study Group; Workshop
Meetings   ➤ Business Meeting; Club/Group Meeting; Convention

➢ Dorm/House Meeting; Informational Meeting
Music/Arts
➢ Audition; Concert; Exhibit; Jam Session; Listening Party; Opening
➢ Performance; Preview; Recital; Rehearsal
Sports
➢ Pep Rally; Pick-Up; Sporting Event; Sporting Practice; Tournament
Trips
➢ Camping Trip; Daytrip; Group Trip; Roadtrip
Other
➢ Carnival; Ceremony; Festival; Flea Market

d. Description

The description of your event is the second most important section apart from the tagline. With the description you can not only give detail about your event, but also add parameters and restrictions. For example, you may want to give a past history of prior events. If this is an annual affair, let Facebook know about the traditions. For sporting events give past scores and times to build anticipation of the score or time to beat. Did your team win last year? Give the score. With your event description you have unlimited characters in which to give the details of why everyone should attend.

REMEMBER DRESS CODE & GIFT OPTIONS

If there is a dress code for your event, remember to place it in the Description for all to read. If it's a birthday party, be sure to state whether gifts are permitted.

e. Privacy Options

Privacy is key when creating an event. You need to give out only as much as will make the event a success and not an ounce more. Remember not to give out more info than you are comfortable giving on your profile. That being said, near the bottom of the event info screen are key privacy settings. They are enabled as the default.

Event Privacy Options Table 8.C
➢ Let guests know they can bring friends to the event; Show the guest list
➢ Enable The Wall; Enable photos; Allow all members to upload photos

If you are having an event with only a few invitees, but still want to show it off to Facebookers, ensure you uncheck the privacy options. Keep in mind that if you enable photos, which is the default setting, *anyone* can post a photo that will be shown on the front page of your event.

EMAIL, PHONE AND STREET ADDRESS NOT REQUIRED

If your invite list is big, you may not want to give out your email address and phone number. These are also not required by Facebook when entering event info.

You also have three access privacy options. These are arguably your most important event privacy options in that they regulate who can sign up for the event and even whether it is secret. Shhh!

Access	Description
Open	Anyone can see the event, join and post to the event's profile. Event appears in search results.
Closed	Only invitees are on the guest list. Anyone can view the event, but only invitees can view the location, guest list, The Wall, photos and comments. Event appears in search results.
Secret	Only invitees can see the event, which does not appear in search results.

SHOUT IT FROM THE DIGITAL MOUNTAIN

Publicize is checked at the bottom of the page (this is the default) so the event will be displayed in search results, when browsing events, and on the Networks page. This is overridden if your event is Secret.

3. Event Guests

After you have inputted your event info, you can check the status of guests invited to attend your event. You have six categories in which to define your invited guests.

This is especially important when you have a large event guest list. This will enable you to get a quick snapshot of who will be there.

4. Exporting Events

Facebook gives you tons of options regarding events. It even has a nifty way for you to export events to third party programs. Select Export Events at the top of your screen.

When you do, you will be presented with detailed instructions for exporting *any* event to popular organizers and calendars like iCal for the Mac, Google Calendar or Microsoft Outlook. You can export an individual event by clicking the export icon below the photo for the event or Facebook will generate a unique URL for downloading your events.

You can easily tell friends about events by selecting the Share icon below any event photo when viewing it.

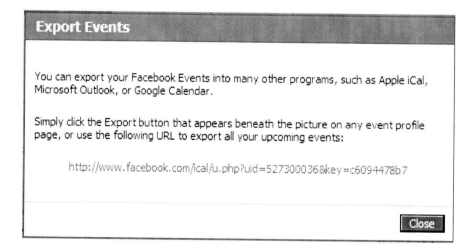

Export Events

You can export your Facebook Events into many other programs, such as Apple iCal, Microsoft Outlook, or Google Calendar.

Simply click the Export button that appears beneath the picture on any event profile page, or use the following URL to export all your upcoming events:

http://www.facebook.com/ical/u.php?uid=527300036&key=c6094478b7

Close

Tip

SCHOOL MASCOT PHOTOS ARE POPULAR
If you have a pet that looks like your school mascot when put in a school colors sweater, submit this photo. Of course, this is tough if your mascot is a wolverine or badger!

B. Facebook Flyers

Instead of stapling flyers to telephone poles and bulletin boards around your school or university, use Facebook Flyers to do it the digital way. Not only will your flyer reach many more people, but they are better for the environment! When setting up an event just click on the provided flyer link.

Alternatively, you can visit Facebook's page for flyers by pointing your browser to www.facebook.com/flyers.php. Flyers have images. Flyers have text. Flyers are hyperlinked. Flyers are cool. All this begs the question: On what networks on Facebook can you advertise? The answer is the schools network in general. You can advertise to your school or *any* other school even if you never attended there! Before you begin, visit the Flyer Board to receive an idea of other flyers on Facebook at: facebook.com/flyer_board.php. Each school within Facebook has its own flyer board.

This is all fine and good, but how much do flyers cost? How about $5 USD for displaying your flyer 10,000 times! That's right, if you display a flyer at your school it costs $5 for 10,000 impressions. If you display it at another school, it costs $5 for 2,500 impressions, which is still a good price. Here are the 10 general flyer categories.

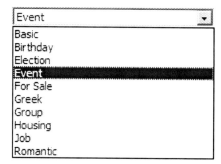

On flyers you are limited to 25 total characters in your title and 200 characters in the body. No HTML can be inserted. As a flyer privacy option, you can pick whether your name will be displayed in the flyer. You also have the option to post to students or everyone on Facebook. The choice is yours. Last, be sure to pick when the flyer will begin showing impressions. You can even choose the start time. Make it at a time when the most people will be online to view your flyer and that are in your target audience. If your friends are in class at 3 pm on Thursday, don't start the ad until after class.

Got a funny photo of a friend who you want to Embarrass on their 21st birthday? If so, flyers are a great way to do it!

60 Second Summary

Key Event and Flyer Tips

- Remember dress code and gift options in the event description
- Use taglines effectively to buzz your event before it starts
- Search local events when traveling
- To get more profile clicks, post on The Wall even if you cannot make it to the event
- Facebook Flyers cost $5 USD for 10,000 impressions at your school and $5 USD for 2,500 at any other school

What You'll Experience

Top Group Rules

Group Privacy Settings

Make a Group Secret. Shhh!

How to Create a Group

IX   Groups

A. Intro to Groups

Groups are online meeting places for likeminded people. They are a great place to post comments and get tons of new friends. On Facebook people start their own groups by creating profiles dedicated to their topic of interest. There are many groups on Facebook covering every topic under the sun and a few under the moon, too. To get started, simply click on the Groups link in the upper left-hand column of your profile and follow the instructions.

👥 Groups

Then you will be presented with groups recently joined by your friends and those you have recently updated. At the top of the screen you can click over to your groups, browse groups, and create a new one.

1. My Groups

If you are a member of a lot of groups, Facebook makes it easy for you to see links to them all in one place. Just select My Groups.

You can easily click over to your groups from here. And if you have not joined any groups yet, don't worry. At the bottom of the screen you are presented with links to start a new group or search for an existing one.

2. Browsing Groups

It's fun to peruse through groups in your networks. Just click on Browse Groups at the top of your screen to be taken to page-after-page of groups. Many of them will be local if you registered your city as a network.

Beneath the group photo is presented three important links: View Discussion Board, Join this Group, and Report Group.

CHECK OUT THE GLOBAL NETWORK
Click the arrow under Network and you can pick the Other network, which is Global. This is great to see hot groups worldwide that may be of interest.

While you see titles for each discussion group on the group's profile, clicking on the View Discussion Board link will show snippets of posts. You can Join this Group by selecting the link or search for more by inputting a search query in the Search for Groups box on the group homepage.

Search for Groups

One of the best ways to search is for a topic of interest. You will be surprised at the number of groups that appear. Winnow it down from there. Once you find a group of interest, just click it and you will be taken to the group's profile. There you will learn detailed information about the group like the admins, members, information, and topics on the discussion board.

How to Report a Group on Facebook Table 9.A
➢ Login → Click on groups → Browse or search for group of interest ➢ Click on group photo → Under the group photo click on Report Group

On each group page you will be able to see profile photos of the group's members. Six photos are displayed on the profile at any one time. Just like friends on a normal profile, Facebook rotates them.

POST ON THE WALL
It's easy for your photo to get lost in a group if there are tons of members. To get your photo noticed, post to The Wall of a group on a frequent basis.

3. Creating an Group

Creating a group on Facebook can be almost as fun as the group itself. Click on Create a New Group and begin the three-step process where you input group info, photo and members.

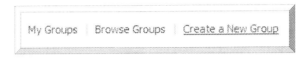

Here are key Facebook group tips when creating a group that will make your outing a success before it even beings.

a. Title

The title is the first written introduction to your group. Make sure it is on point and does not ramble. You have plenty of space in the description section to disclose why your group is cool. Try to limit your title to five words or less. Facebook gives you 75 characters in which to title your group, including spaces. Within reason, your group name can be anything you want. Facebook does not, however, allow you to place HTML in a group's name.

b. Categories and Types

There are eight different group categories on Facebook. Within each are numerous subcategories. Here's a listing for each, and, of course, party has the most subcategories!

Group Categories & Types Table 9.B

Business
  ➤ Companies; Consumer Groups; Employment & Work; General
  ➤ Home Business; Investing; Marketing & Advertising; Public Relations
  ➤ Real Estate

Common Interest
  ➤ Activities; Age; Beauty; Beliefs & Causes; Current Events
  ➤ Dating & Relationships; Families; Food & Drink; Friends; Gardening
  ➤ Health & Wellness; History; Hobbies & Crafts; Languages
  ➤ Pets & Animals; Philosophy; Politics; Religion & Spirituality; Science
  ➤ Self-Help; Sexuality; Travel; Wine

Entertainment & Arts

➢ Books & Literature; Celebrities; Comics & Animation; Dance ➢ Fashion; Fine Arts; General; Humor; Movies; Nightlife; Online Media ➢ Performing Arts; Radio; Television; Theatre
Geography ➢ Cities; Countries; General; Neighborhoods; Places; Regions ➢ Ridesharing & Transportation; States
Internet & Technology ➢ Computers & Hardware; Cyberculture; Gadgets; Gaming; General ➢ Languages & Formats; Mobile; Multimedia; News; Software ➢ Websites
Just for Fun ➢ Facebook Classics; Fan Clubs; Inside Jokes; Outlandish Statements ➢ Too Much Information; Totally Pointless; Totally Random
Music ➢ Blues; Classical; Country; Dance; Electronic; Folk; General; Indie ➢ Instruments; International; Jazz; Latin; Live Music; Metal ➢ R&B Soul; Rap & Hip Hop; Reggae; Religious; Rock; Songwriting
Organizations ➢ Academic Organizations; Advocacy Organizations; Clubs & Societies ➢ Community Organizations; General; Non-Profit Organizations ➢ Philanthropic Organizations; Political Organizations ➢ Professional Organizations; Religious Organizations ➢ Volunteer Organizations
Sports & Recreation ➢ Automotive & Racing; Cheerleading; College Sports; Dance ➢ Extreme Sports; Fantasy Sports; Fitness & Exercise ➢ Gambling; Games; General Sports; High School Sports ➢ International Sports; Intramural Sports; Martial Arts; Olympic Sports ➢ Outdoor Sports; Professional Sports; Recreational Sports; ➢ Sports Leagues; Water Sports; Weightlifting & Bodybuilding
Student Groups

c. Description

The description of your group is the second most important section apart from the title. Within the description you can not only give detail about your group, but also add parameters and restrictions. For example, you may want to give a past history of prior groups (what worked and what did not) and set the ground rules.

Top Group Rules Table 9.C
➢ No spamming members
➢ No advertising products
➢ New members: Do not announce yourself as being new, but instead get involved by posting
➢ No joining the group just to get people to join your own group
➢ Pimp the group by showing you are a member on your Facebook profile
➢ Keep posts relevant and to the point
➢ Be civil or be removed

With your group description you have unlimited characters in which to give the details of why your group is the coolest. Hint: Say it has the hippest members. Like your group title, Facebook does not allow you to place HTML in a group's description section. In this area you need to start developing the theme of your group immediately.

TELL WHERE THE GROUP IS BASED

It is a good idea to input the location of your group. Remember that this is the group address. It does not have to be your own. If you live in Wichita, Kansas, but are starting a group about the Big Apple, the city should be New York.

Unlike with events, you are not given taglines to use for groups . . . at least in a formal sense. By using keywords in your description you can snag many more new members than with a normal group description. Buzz your group before it starts. You have unlimited characters for your description so don't be shy. Place keywords that pertain to the group at the very bottom of the description section. Set them off with a term so that visitors know why they are present. For instance, "Fast Car Group Keywords: V-8, Tire Slicks, Stick Shift, Porsche, Dual Overhead Cams, Fuel Injectors, etc."

d. Photo Upload

Your group photo is vital. If it is a bad photo or does not fit well with the theme of your group, you will not get many members. Upload a high quality, relevant photo and remember that you have a 4 MB size limit.

Like all photos on Facebook, group photos are limted to .jpg, .gif and .png files.

e. Members

Adding a new member is easy. Facebook provides a search box so you can track them down on the site. You can also see those that have not yet replied to the invite and those you have blocked for whatever reason.

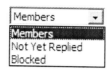

f. Privacy Options

Privacy is key when creating a group. You need to give out only as much as will make the group a success and not an ounce more. Remember not to give out more info than you are comfortable giving on your profile regardless of whether you are the admin of the group or simply a member posting info. That being said, near the bottom of the group info screen are key privacy settings. They are enabled as the default.

Group Privacy Options Table 9.D
➢ Show related groups ➢ Enable discussion board ➢ Enable The Wall ➢ Enable photos ➢ Allow all members to upload photos

If you want to create a group with only a few select members, but still want to show it off to Facebookers, ensure you uncheck the options above. Keep in mind that if you enable photos, which is the default setting, *anyone* can post a photo that will be shown on the front page of your group. You also have three access privacy options. These are arguably your most important group privacy options in that they regulate who can sign up for the group and even whether it is secret. Shhh! Do you want potential new members to have to ask the group's moderator

You can easily tell friends about groups by selecting the Share icon below any group photo when viewing it.

(that would be you) to join? This gives you the option of checking out their Facebook profile *before* letting them in the door. On the other hand, you will not have as many Facebookers join your group if it is private. It is also a lot of work if you get tons of join requests.

Access	Description
Open	Anyone can see the group, join and post to the group's profile. Group appears in search results.
Closed	The administrator must okay any new members. Anyone can view the group, but only members can view The Wall, photos and comments. Group appears in search results.
Secret	Only members can see the group, which does not appear in search results. Membership is by invitation only. Think of this as your invite-only party!

SHOUT IT FROM THE DIGITAL MOUNTAIN

Check publicize at the bottom of the page (this is the default) so that your group will be displayed in search results, when browsing groups, and on the networks page. This will be overridden if your group is set to secret.

If you remove yourself as the last member of a group (i.e., you are the admin), the group will be deleted. In this case you will be the last one to jump off the sinking group ship.

g. Group Posts

When you post, the time is date stamped and your Facebook name is highlighted. Anyone who clicks on your name will be taken to your profile. Your photo is also shown next to your post link and it is another way for people to visit your profile. When clicked on, readers can view your comments, see your default photo, and view your profile. This is a great way to drive traffic to your profile by other likeminded Facebookers who are interested in the same stuff.

If you post a comment in a group where you are in over your head about the subject, you will get little to no clicks over to your profile and even less friend requests. This is especially true in private groups. Questions, however, are usually welcomed as long as they are not too lame.

What's more, when you post a comment, your name will be exclusively shown on the row for that category and it *stays* there until another person posts. What a great way to get Facebook exposure! Start a cool topic and watch the clicks roll in. There is hardly any limit to the crazy topics allowed under Facebook groups.

If you can find a group with slow posts, your post (and link to your profile) will stay up the longest time and increase the number of clicks to your profile.

60 Second Summary

Key Group Tips

- No HTML in the title or group description
- Group photos are limited to 4 MB in size
- Post to The Wall often in groups with lots of members to get profile clicks
- In groups with few postings, your post will be viewed longer, but will not get as many eyeballs
- Secret groups are not shown in search results and are invite only

What You'll Experience

Access Facebook from a Cellphone

Facebook Mobile Privacy Settings

Upload Cellphone Photos Directly to Facebook

Text Friends from Cellphone

X   Facebook Mobile

A. Facebook Mobile Introduction

Facebook Mobile is a great communication tool that spans the world and lets you access Facebook anywhere you have cellphone access. With it you can view your profile, browse Facebook, post to your notes, send messages, poke friends, and upload new photos all from your cellphone. Oh, and did we mention it's all free except for any cellphone service charges you may incur? Below we'll discuss Facebook Mobile tips for getting the most out of your Facebook experience when away from your computer.

Mobile

To get started click "more" in the left-hand column of your profile → select the Mobile link. This will take you to the mobile page of your profile.

B. Friends' Uploads

Not only does Facebook let you keep in touch with friends on the road, but you can also view uploads by friends while *they* are on the road. Click on Friends' Uploads at the top of the page.

This is also the default page of your mobile profile that displays uploads from fiends' Facebook mobile accounts. How is this useful? Let's say your friend is at a concert or sporting event that you have to miss. Here is where you can find the cool photos they are beaming back to Facebook from their cellphone. If you are just getting started on Facebook Mobile, this is a good area to get ideas of how your friends have used Facebook mobile when out and about.

C. Phonebook

Your phonebook is logically under the Facebook Mobile area of your profile. If you want to view a friend's number, look here first before poking them. Annoying friends will soon be ex-friends. Select the middle option at the top of your Facebook Mobile page.

You can then easily look up a name by alphabetical listing. Start typing a friend's name and Facebook will pull up their phone information automatically

D. Account Settings

Your mobile account settings are the area where you can really make things happen on Facebook Mobile. Select Account Settings from the top to get started.

You will be presented with a key Website and email addresses that enable you to browse Facebook on your cellphone, upload photos right to your photo albums and text to your Facebook notes.

| Settings | Networks | Notifications | Mobile |

Here are the addresses you must remember. Program them in your cellphone now before you forget.

Type	Address	Description
Mobile Web	m.Facebook.com	Browse Facebook
Mobile Uploads	photos@facebook.com	Upload Photos from Cellphone
Mobile Uploads	notes@facebook.com	Text to Profile Notes
Mobile Text	Your Cellphone Number	Reply to and Send Messages, Pokes & Posts

The Web address m.facebook.com is actually a mobile version of Facebook. This is similar to .mobi extension Web addresses, such as www.facebook.mobi.

MUST TURN ON MOBILE TEXT

Once you have established you cellphone number with Facebook Mobile, you must still turn on Mobile Text. Click "more" → Mobile → Account Settings → Turn on Mobile Text.

1. Mobile Web

Click on Mobile Web under Account Settings and you will be taken to an overview of what Facebook Mobile looks like on your cellphone. The graphics are sparse, but the meat of the matter is there for *all* sections of your profile. Even photos are included. Mobile Web is where you can surf your Facebook profile at will. Always be connected!

Did we mention that you can also stay in touch with the Events portion of Facebook? This is essential when on the road and you want to know what is happening in your area. Below is an example of a cellphone screen listing up and coming events.

Events Screen on Mobile Phone

2. Mobile Uploads

What are Mobile Uploads? They are the coolest and quickest way to get info onto your Facebook profile when traveling. Did you take a great photo on your cellphone at the skate park? If so, zap it to Facebook. Want to send a blurb to Notes about the U2 concert while you are at it? No problem. On Facebook it's easy. Just click on Uploads to use this powerful feature.

There you are presented with two key email addresses: photos@facebooks.com is the first one and notes@facebook.com is the second. When you sign up for the service, Facebook will send you a unique code after they get your email. You must then enter your code on the site. Once the correct code is inputted, you do not have to enter another one.

Test your cellphone by your computer and input the one-time code so that you will have no trouble from the road.

3. Mobile Texts

The acronym SMS stands for Short Message Service, which is a fancy way to say *text messaging* on a cellphone. Most of us have received text messages before, either on the computer or a cellphone. If so, you are used to seeing cryptic letter and number combinations like: C U L8R, LUV U 2 DTH, and NP (no problem). SMS lingo is like vanity license plates run amok and it is *cool*, if you know how to play the game. To get in the game, conduct an Internet search on "best license plates" or "popular license plates" to get an idea of alternate lingo you can use. Mobile Texts on Facebook allow you to poke friends, post to The Wall, write a Note, search for, and add friends. Think of Mobile Texts as your Facebook command center for staying in touch anywhere in the world. Click on Texts and get your opposable thumbs loosened up.

Below is a search for Facebook's founder, Mark Zuckerberg, as it would look on a cellphone.

Events Screen on Mobile Phone

You can conduct your Facebook business by texting to FBOOK, which are the numbers 32665. Keep in mind that you can always text friends on Facebook even if they don't have a cellphone since your messages go right to their Facebook profile.

Action	Command	Example Text
Add a Friend	Add	Add Bob Marks
Fire a Friend	Fire	Fire Bob Marks
Get Cell Number	Cell	Cell Bob Marks
Message	Msg	Msg Bob Marks Are You Ready
Poke	Poke	Poke Bob Marks
Search Profile	N/A	Bob Marks
Wall Post	Wall	Wall Bob Marks Ace Your Exam
Write a Note	Note	Note Bob Marks Check Out www.bottletreebooks.com

TLK-2-U-L8R (Talk to you later) is a good example of a message or note you can send from your cell. Here are two of our favorites: JUADLAM (Jumping up and down like a monkey) and ROR (Raffing out loud), which is a Scooby Doo-ism! Check out other great text shorthand at netlingo.com.

TEXT FRIENDS IN A FOREIGN LANGUAGE

What's really cool is to have your message translated into another language. Google has over 115 languages that it translates, including Klingon and Elmer Fudd! Check it out: http://www.google.com/language_tools.

Smilies work great in text messages. The most basic is the smiley face :-) or the wink face ;-) that is created by the semicolon, hyphen and closed parenthesis. There are tons of great ones at netlingo.com including :--.) for Cindy Crawford; (-8^(1) for Homer Simpson; and |:-) for the dreaded unibrow. How about }:-k> for Fidel Castro?

ENSURE CELLPHONE NUMBER IS CONFIRMED

At the top of the Mobile Texts screen your cellphone number should be listed. If it is not, you must confirm it with Facebook before using the mobile settings.

60 Second Summary

Key Facebook Mobile Tips

- There is no charge for using Facebook mobile apart from connection charges your cellphone company may charge you
- You only have to register your cellphone once with Facebook
- When you upload a photo or note to your profile for the first time, you must input a unique code you are provided, which only has to be done the first time
- Photos@facebook.com is the email address to send photos from a cellphone
- Notes@facebook.com is the email address to post profile notes from a cellphone
- FBOOK is where to send text commands from a cellphone

What You'll Experience

Post Videos & Songs

Posted Item Limitations

Share Anything on the Internet

Control Who Sees Posted Items

XI   Posted Items

A. Overview

Posted Items are a great way to show fellow Facebookers cool things you've found on the Web. You can link to Notes, Websites, photos, songs and even videos. That's not all. You can even post content from within Facebook like a groovy profile or Notes of a friend. You can even post entire profiles. The possibilities are endless and this is a good way to get new friends by turning them on to areas of the Web that would be of interest! Posted Items are hidden on your profile. To get to them, click on the down arrow in the left-hand column → Posted Items.

⬚ Posted Items

Posted Items are displayed on your profile in a designated area. Visitors can see all of your posted items by clicking on the handy link.

You can select "edit" at any time and delete any of your posted items. To delete all your posted items at once, just click the x in the upper right-hand corner. Remember to include items that mostly relate to the theme of your profile.

B. Posting Items within Facebook

Finding and posting great content from within Facebook can be employed in just a few steps. We've all seen those "Share on Facebook" buttons scattered around the site.

Click share button → "Post to Profile" tab. This will automatically copy and paste the Facebook content onto your profile under the Posted Items section. Any comments you have made about Posted Items will also be included and the default will be that anyone who can view your profile can view your Posted Items. Be aware that friends will be able to comment on your posted items, and in many ways that is a major point of the exercise.

C. Posting Items Outside of Facebook

Turning the Facebook world on to cool things the Web has to offer is a great way to keep your existing friends and attract even more. Posting Items of interest is a great way to make your profile "sticky". In other words, if your friends can get the info on your page, why go anywhere else? What's more, you can leave comments about your postings for friends to read. Let's now take a look at the various ways to post Websites, photos, music and videos to your profile.

Facebook does not allow you to place HTML in the comments portion of items posted.

1. URL Link

If you find a groovy Website just copy and paste its URL into the "Post a link" URL window and hit Post. In Microsoft's Internet Explorer, Apple's Safari, and Mozilla's FireFox just click once in the browser's URL window and the entire window will be highlighted → right click → select copy → return to Facebook → right click → select paste. Erase the extra "http://". Easy enough.

Post a link

http://

Post

When you post a Website URL, the title of the Website is also imported onto your profile, which provides a brief overview of the page visitors are about to see when they click on the link.

a. Music Posts

Great music is vital to any popular Facebook profile. You can go on for paragraphs in your interest section about bands you love, but allowing visitors to actually hear music from them takes it to a whole other level. If you attract new friends because of your Led Zeppelin-themed profile, you may want to have the latest

Follow this link to view tens of thousands of artists giving music away for free: http://www.goingware.com/tips/legal-downloads.html#intro.

Wolfmother song in your playlist to introduce friends to the power trio rock band that has a similar sound. There are a number of ways to go about it. The first is to look for a link on the music site. A number of unsigned bands will provide this link to distribute their music for free. If there is a link, copy and paste it into the box at the top of the Posted Items page. Then click on Share. When the share box appears, select "Post to Profile" and click "Post".

Besides the HTML freedom Facebook gives you in various areas like Notes to insert limited HTML codes, there is a little-know application that has been developed on the Facebook Platform specifically for HTML. It's much more powerful than normal Facebook HTML. In fact, using it will allow you to play mp3 files right on your profile. Where do you find this powerful elixir? Just follow this link and type "HTML Box" into the search window.

facebook.com/apps/?ref=wn

Choose your HTML Box privacy settings and add the application to your profile. Once you do, it's easy to place videos and music onto your profile. Once you have found an mp3 URL on the Web, insert it into the HTML below and place it in your HTML Box. You can also include the artist's name, album photo and song title.

<fb:mp3 src="URL" height="###" width="###" artist="ARTIST NAME" title="SONG TITLE" album="URL FOR ALBUM COVER"/>

If you want to add colors and backgrounds into your HTML Box, remember the Four Color Rule. What is often mistakenly called the "Three Color Rule" is actually a guideline for applying background and foreground Web colors. Specifically, the rule states that one background color (preferably pale) should be used in conjunction with only three foreground colors, hence the more aptly titled "Four Color Rule". More than a subtle use of multiple background colors will hamper reading of the foreground colors. Colored text, even if it is black or white, will use up one of your targeted three foreground colors. Borders use up the other colors. The remaining fourth color will be your profile background color.

Avoid Closely-Related Colors

Facebook requires that you use your real name. You do not, however, have to include your full last name. The first letter of your last name will suffice and you can put your nickname between your first and last names. Tones that are closely related, for example: yellows-and-greens, reds-and-greens, etc., are "vibrating" colors. The human eye has difficulty distinguishing between the two. This is especially the case for "color blind" Internet users. Avoid use of these vibrating colors.

b. Photo Posts

If you find a photo on the Web that you want to post, there are a few steps you must follow. Keep in mind that photos vie for attention on the Web. Many times just posting a link to a Website will force your profile visitors to search up and down the site to find the photo. There is a much better way and that is by providing a direct post on your profile. Did you know each photo on the Web has its own unique URL? Here is how to find and post them.

Post Photo URLs Table 11.A
➤ Find a photo on the Web → Right click on photo → Select "Properties"
➤ Copy and paste the displayed URL into Facebook Posted Items
➤ Click "Post" and you are finished

Keep content on your Facebook profile fresh. That means you should change your photos, videos, and profile information once in awhile. Add new posts and delete old ones. Your profile should live and breathe and change since it is an extension of yourself.

c. Video Posts

When you post a video, the video's description will be shown on your profile and a hyperlink created that is the same as the link you posted. How do you find video URLs? It's easy. Did you find the world's coolest video on YouTube and want to put in on your Facebook profile? No problem. Even if a video is not on Facebook, we will show you how to get it on *your* profile from the Web's most popular video site.

Similar to the photos you show on your profile, swap out your posted videos once in a while to keep your profile fresh and visitors coming back for more.

Google-owned YouTube has taken the Internet by storm . . . video storm that is. YouTube is so popular it is becoming an adjective in the English language and is the leading site for the coolest videos. It has hundreds of thousands of videos ready for linking. You do not have to set up an account with YouTube to post videos from the site onto your Facebook profile. Most of the videos are free and created by people just like you. If you find a rad video on YouTube.com, getting it onto your profile is very similar to showing a video already on Facebook. Table 11.B show how to post YouTube videos in a few steps.

Post YouTube Videos **Table 11.B**
➢ Find a video on YouTube.com ➢ Click on the initial screen of the video and you'll be taken to the YouTube profile where the video is displayed ➢ Next to the video is the About This Video block.

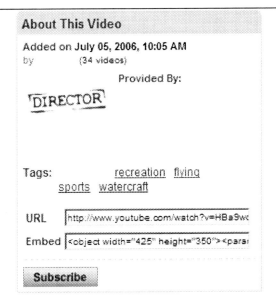

> ➤ Copy the URL by clicking anywhere in the rectangle and then select Copy by right clicking your mouse
> ➤ Now go to Facebook and paste the URL into the Posted Items URL box
> ➤ Click on "Post"

d. Email Videos to Friends

Have you ever run across a video on the Web and wished you could show it to a friend? This happens all the time, but many people do not realize you can email videos to your Facebook friends with a few clicks of the mouse. You can always just copy the video URL and email that link to your friends from a third party email client such as Gmail. Since it is a hyperlink, all they have to do is click on the link to be taken to the Facebook profile where the video is showing. Below we'll show you how to email videos from the Web's most popular video sites.

e. Email YouTube Videos

YouTube makes it easy to share videos on its site via email. Let's get to it.

Email YouTube Videos Table 11.C
➤ Find a video on www.YouTube.com ➤ Click on the initial screen of the video and you'll be taken to the YouTube profile where the video is displayed ➤ Click on Share Video beneath the screen

- ➤ An email launch screen will pop up
- ➤ Type in your email addresses, message, name, and click Send
- ➤ A thumbnail of the video and link will be sent to your friends

NO SUBJECT HEADING OPTION

YouTube does not give you the option of adding an email heading. Instead, it inserts the default subject heading: "XX sent you a video!" where "XX" is either your name or "somebody" if you do not insert a name. YouTube also automatically inserts "This video is awesome!" as the default email message, which you can change.

You can always copy the URL shown next to the video and email or IM that link to your friends. Since it is a hyperlink, all they have to do is click on the link to be taken to the YouTube profile where the video is showing.

Be sure to include a link to your Facebook profile when emailing video links from third party sites.

f. Email Videos from Google Video

Google makes it easy to share videos, but it takes a click or two more than with YouTube.

Email Google Videos **Table 11.D**
➤ Find a video at www.video.google.com ➤ Click on the thumbnail of the video and you'll be taken to the Google profile where the video is displayed ➤ Click the "Email – Note – Post to Facebook" button next to the video   ➤ An email launch screen is displayed → Type in email addresses and message ➤ Click Send Link → A thumbnail of the video and link will be sent to friends

<u>No Subject Heading Option</u>

Google does not give you the option of adding a heading. Instead, it inserts the default subject heading: "Watch VIDEO TITLE HERE on Google Video." Google also automatically inserts the description of the video within the email message, which you cannot change.

Getting the video URL link to email or IM it to your friends is a bit tricky with Google Video. The URL link is not displayed next to the video like it is in YouTube. Right-clicking on the video will not display the URL link since the videos are in ShockWave format. Therefore, you have to do it the old fashioned way.

Email Google Video URL Link **Table 11.E**
➤ Find a video at www.video.google.com ➤ Click on the video thumbnail and you'll be taken to the Google profile where the video is displayed ➤ Copy the URL link from the Address section or your Internet browser Address http://video.google.com/videoplay?docid=-3934788900   Go ➤ Email the video URL link to your friends

g. Email Videos from Yahoo Video

With Yahoo Video you can easily email videos to your Facebook friends. Here are the quick steps.

Email Yahoo Videos **Table 11.F**
➢ Find a video on www.video.yahoo.com ➢ Click on the initial screen of the video and you'll be taken to the Yahoo profile where the video is displayed ➢ Click the Email button at the bottom of the video

➢ An email launch screen will be displayed ➢ Type in your email addresses, message, name, and click Send ➢ A thumbnail of the video and link will be sent to your friends

NO SUBJECT HEADING CHANGES

Like Google, Yahoo Video does not give you the option of adding an email heading. Instead, it inserts the default heading: "Check out VIDEO TITLE on Yahoo Video."

h. Email Videos from AOL Video

AOL has built a lot of functionality into its video engine. Here's how you can email its videos.

Email AOL Videos **Table 11.G**
➢ Find a video at www.video.aol.com ➢ Click on E-mail This
Notify AOL   IM This   E-mail This   Tag This
➢ This will launch your default email program and insert a link to the video in the email message

Getting the video URL link to email your Facebook friends is a bit tricky with AOL Video. The URL link is not displayed next to the video like it is in YouTube. Right-clicking on the video will not display the URL link since the videos are in ShockWave format.

Email AOL Video URL Link Table 11.H
➢ Find a video at www.video.aol.com
➢ Click on the thumbnail of the video and you'll be taken to the AOL profile where the video is displayed
➢ Copy the URL link from the Address section of your Internet browser
Address http://uncutvideo.aol.com/Playback.do?AssetID=fb5e4   ✓ ➡ Go
➢ Email the video URL link to your friends

LIKE A VIDEO? ADD IT TO YOUR FAVORITES LIST

Facebook makes it easy to add a video to your favorites list so you easily find it again, just add it to your profile. No more searching for the videos of your choice. You can even send them to friends. What could be easier?

If you find a video on Facebook you feel may violate Facebook's Terms of Use, you can flag the video for review.

2. Partner "Share on Facebook" Buttons

Facebook enables you to create "Share on Facebook" buttons that allow Web content to be displayed on your profile. Just click on one of the buttons, select "Post on Facebook" and click "Post". You will also have the option of emailing the link to friends. Realize that if you email the link, friends can reply and tell you what they think.

3. Bookmarklet

Facebook allows you to download a powerful Internet browser plug-in called a bookmarklet. What this does is really create a portable "Share on Facebook" link that can be used for any content you find on the Web. The bookmarklet will automatically generate a share box for you. Just select "Post on Facebook" and click "Post".

> Be sure to visit the privacy chapter of *Facebook Fanatic* to learn how to lock down the privacy of your Posted Items.

Getting a bookmarklet on your browser is easy. On the right side of your Posted Items main page you will see a "Share on Facebook" button → right click → Pick "Add to Favorites" → Select "Create in" → choose "Links" folder. When you take these steps, the "Share on Facebook" button will appear at the top of you browser.

4. Share Content from Your Website

Facebook provides three HTML lines of codes that you can copy and paste into the HTML of your Website to create a link to Facebook. When a Facebooker sees the link, all they have to do is click on it to have the content shown as a Posted Item on their profile. This is a great way to spread news articles or to buzz a book. Simply replace the bolded 'url' designation with the URL where your content resides such as demonstrated at www.bottletreebooks.com/facebook.htm.

Text Hyperlink

```
<script>function fbs_click() {u=location.href;t=document.title;window.open('
http://www.facebook.com/sharer.php?u='+encodeURIComponent(u)+'&t='+encodeURI
Component(t),'sharer','toolbar=0,status=0,width=626,height=436');return
false;}</script><a href=" http://www.facebook.com/share.php?u=<url>"
onclick="return fbs_click()" target="_blank">Share on Facebook</a>
```

Image Link

```
<script>function fbs_click() {u=location.href;t=document.title;window.open('
http://www.facebook.com/sharer.php?u='+encodeURIComponent(u)+'&t='+encodeURI
Component(t),'sharer','toolbar=0,status=0,width=626,height=436');return
false;}</script><style> html .fb_share_link { padding:2px 0 0 20px; height:16px;
background:url(
http://static.ak.facebook.com/images/share/facebook_share_icon.gif?11:26981) no-
repeat top left; }</style><a href=" http://www.facebook.com/share.php?u=<url>"
```

onclick="return fbs_click()" target="_blank" class="fb_share_link">Share on Facebook</a>

Stylized Image Link

<script>function fbs_click() {u=location.href;t=document.title;window.open(' http://www.facebook.com/sharer.php?u='+encodeURIComponent(u)+'&t='+encodeURI Component(t),'sharer','toolbar=0,status=0,width=626,height=436');return false;}</script><style> html .fb_share_button { display: -moz-inline-block; display:inline-block; padding:1px 20px 0 5px; height:15px; border:1px solid #d8dfea; background:url(http://static.ak.facebook.com/images/share/facebook_share_icon.gif?11:26981) no-repeat top right; } html .fb_share_button:hover { color:#fff; border-color:#295582; background:#3b5998 url(http://static.ak.facebook.com/images/share/facebook_share_icon.gif?11:26981) no-repeat top right; text-decoration:none; } </style> <a href=" http://www.facebook.com/share.php?u=**url**" class="fb_share_button" onclick="return fbs_click()" target="_blank" style="text-decoration:none;">Share</a>

The minor problem with sharing content using the HTML above is that it only provides a link. There are no meta tags that tell Facebook what *type* of content it is (audio, video, image, text, etc.). Add the following basic tags to ensure the title of your content and a short description are imported into Facebook. This also includes the initial image of your content, if it is an image or video, which is displayed on Facebook

Meta Tags

<meta name="title" content="'Entire Tales & Poems of Edgar Allan Poe' book published by BottleTree" />
<meta name="description" content="Photographic and annotated edition of all of Edgar Allan Poe's poems and stories. Experience the master of the short story as you never have before." />
<link rel="image_src" href="http://www.bottletreebooks.com/EntireTales.jpg" />

Per Facebook:

Multimedia Tags

The ideal way for you to connect videos and media files to the share link is to make the URL in the link point to an html page that contains the <meta>/<link> tags described above (title, description, image_src) along with the some additional <meta>/<link> tags:

Audio (required)
<meta name="title" content="page_title" />
<meta name="description" content="audio_description" />
<link rel="image_src" href="audio_image_src url (eg. cover image)" />
<link rel="audio_src" href="audio_src url" />
<meta name="audio_type" content="Content-Type header field" />

Audio (optional)
<meta name="audio_title" content="audio_title (eg. song name)" />
<meta name="audio_artist" content="audio_artist_name" />
<meta name="audio_album" content="audio_album_name" />

Video* (required)
<meta name="title" content="video_title" />
<meta name="description" content="video_description" />
<link rel="image_src" href="video_screenshot_image_src url" />
<link rel="video_src" href="video_src url"/>*
<meta name="video_height" content="video_height" />
<meta name="video_width" content="video_width" />
<meta name="video_type" content="Content-Type header field" />

Video (example)
Here is an example of Flash Video that is embed:
<embed src="http://www.example.com/player.swf" flashvars="video_id=123456789" width="300" height="200" type="application/x-shockwave-flash" />
For that video, the appropriate metadata would look like this:
<link rel="video_src" href="http://www.example.com/player.swf?video_id=123456789"/>
<meta name="video_height" content="200" />
<meta name="video_width" content="300" />
<meta name="video_type" content="application/x-shockwave-flash" />

60 Second Summary

Key Posted Items Tips

- Many upstart bands offer free music that you can post on Facebook
- Use bookmarklets to easily post Web content to your Facebook profile
- If you find a cool video outside of Facebook, email it friends
- Add meta tag HTML when sharing content from your site

What You'll Experience

Create & Upload Videos

Add YouTube Videos to Your Profile

Make Money Off Your Videos

Emailing Videos

XII   Videos

A. Videos Introduction

Videos on Facebook have taken off like wildfire and they are one of the best ways to launch your profile into the super popularity atmosphere. Upload a great, original video and you are on your way to Facebook stardom. Video messages can be sent to friends and you can tag them in videos just as you can in photos and Notes. You can even use any of the videos on YouTube's vast network to show on your Facebook profile by employing a secret HTML Box and show multiple videos on your profile.

🎥 Video

The Facebook Video application does not automatically appear on your profile like other applications such as Notes and Marketplace. You must add it yourself. To find the Video application just visit the developers' section of Facebook and you will see the Facebook Video icon on the first or second page. You can also search for it within Facebook.

When you add the Video application you are presented with a number of options regarding how visible you want your application to be. Check the ones you want enabled. The default is that they are all selected. When finished, click on "Add Video" at the bottom of the page and the application will appear on your profile. When added, the application will appear in the left-hand column of your profile under the "more" option.

B. Four Main Components of a Video

Videos on Facebook have four main components other than the video itself: Starter Image, Title, Description, and Tags. Let's discuss how to optimize each so that your videos zoom up the Facebook popularity charts.

> JumpCut.com is a Website that lets you edit video and add music online..

1. Video Starter Image

Think of your starter image as the front door of your video house. It should make people want to come inside and take a look around, have a cup of tea and stay awhile. When you upload a video, Facebook lets you pick the starter image, which serves as the thumbnail for the video. The starter image must grab attention. How many times have you seen blurry, nondescript starter images on Facebook that do not relate to the actual video? Starter Images should also give insight into what the video is about. If the starter image is a basketball court but when the video plays it immediately pans to a car wreck that happened outside the basketball court, it is not relevant to the actual video content. Also, the starter image should have colors that jump off the screen to grab attention. Sparse use of text should be used in the starter image as it is difficult to read on a thumbnail.

Video Starter Image Key Elements Table 12.A
➢ Entice visitors to play video ➢ Few text letters or words ➢ Grab attention, even from a thumbnail view ➢ Relevant to video content ➢ Show vibrant colors

USE A FREE PHOTO AND VIDEO MONTAGE SERVICE

There is a great Website that lets you combine still photos with your videos. The site is onetruemedia.com and with it you can easily add a splashy starter image to your videos. And it is all free!

2. Video Title

Video titles are limited to 65 total characters, including spaces. Your title is the most important part of the video apart from the actual video itself. When someone views the initial image of a video on Facebook it is very difficult to tell if the video will be any good. If your video of the coolest skateboard trick starts off with a pan of trees that your skater is going to jump from, people may think it is a boring video of a nature preserve by merely looking at the initial screen capture. That is why your title is so important. Do not be afraid to use puffery terms such as "coolest" or "radical" or "wildest" or "biggest," etc. You get the picture. Make sure, however, that you do not label a boring video as "wild" or it won't get added to many profiles. If a Facebooker's search term shows up in your video title, they will likely play the video.

	Popular Title Terms Table 12.B	
1980s	Acoustic Guitar	Ads
Animation	Anime	Art
Artist	Awesome	Babies
Best Music	Bollywood	Comedy
Cool	Dance	Dog
Film	Football	For Sale
Fun	Funny	Girls
Guitar	Hilarious	Homes
Humor	Humor	Laughs
Live Music	Japanese Anime	Movie
Movies	Music	Music Video
News	Radical	Real Estate
Sexy	Soccer	Travel
Video Game Screen Shots	Video Game Tricks	Video Games
Videos	Wild	Unreal

3. Video Description

The description of your video is the third most important section behind the actual video itself and the title. Your description is unlimited on Facebook. In it tell who (if anyone) is shown in your video. Also ensure that you tell people what

Make your description a succinct recount of who, what, where and why.

is going to happen, but do not give away the ending if there is a surprise! For instance, "Boy takes a spill" or "Girl gets wet". Since Facebook.com is a worldwide site, it's important to tell *where* your video was shot.

People also want to know *why* your video was shot. Were you scanning a pond on a fishing trip when the trout jumped out of the water and into the boat? Were you videoing a full moon for astronomy class when the UFO flew by? This lends an air of credibility to your video since people will know that it wasn't staged.

USE COMPELLING WORDS
If there is a surprise ending, use call-to-action words, warnings or questions like: "See what happens next!" or "Don't try this at home!" or "Got mud?"

4. Tagging Friends in Videos
On most video sites such as YouTube or AOL Video, tags are nothing more than keywords pertaining to your video so that people searching on those terms can find your video. The more specific your tags, the easier they will be to find but the more limited the number of searchers will be. Facebook adds a new twist by allowing you to tag friends that appear in your videos just like with Notes and photos. This is a unique way to show friends off and get even more friends.

TAG THE MAIN CHARACTERS
A lot of videos have lots of people in them. Be sure, however, to tag the main characters doing the action so people can visit your friends' profiles.

C. Upload Videos
There are three ways to add video to your Facebook profile. The first way is to upload video that is resident on your computer. Next, you can upload from a mobile device such as an iPhone or record a new video from a Camcorder or Webcam. You can also copy the URL of a video already showing on the Internet so that it will play on your profile, but there is a trick to doing this. We will show you ways to accomplish all these methods so that your profile will keep visitors coming back for more and the popularity of your Facebook profile will zoom.

🎥 Create a New Video

Videos added to your profile will be shown if you check the profile box titled: "Make this my Profile Video" when you added the Video application, and you can only show one video at a time. Each newly added video will not replace the one that is

> Videos are limited to 300 MB in size and must be under 15 minutes in length.

currently showing on your profile. You must tell Facebook that you want the video in question to be your profile video from your video page. Videos do not have to be unique to Facebook. If you have uploaded a video onto YouTube or MySpace, you can still upload it onto Facebook. Each time your video is added to a profile, a link is provided to your profile so Facebookers can check out if cool people are adding the video. Because this link is always displayed back to the originator of the video, uploading original videos onto Facebook is a good way to increase your popularity.

1. File to Facebook
Video uploads on Facebook from your computer are easy. Clicking the File Upload link will launch a Facebook page that allows videos to be uploaded from your hardrive.

File Upload	Mobile Video	Record Video

After clicking the link just browse for the file. Then you will be asked to input the title, description and tag friends in your video.

Tip

VIDEO CREATION CONSTRAINTS
Facebook requires that you or your friends have created the video you upload and that one of you also appears in the video. This is so you can tag them and promote your friends.

	Facebook Video Formats Table XII.C	
.3gp	.3gp2	.avi
.dv	.mpg	.mpg4
.mov	.mqv	.wmv
.asf	.wma	

Here are the steps needed to record video and get it loaded onto your computer.

Create and Upload Video to Your Profile Table 12.D
➢ Record video on a video camera ➢ Upload video to computer using a USB or FireWire cable for MiniDV, Digital8, Direct-to-DVD or pure digital camera ➢ Edit video to display only the segment you want to show on the Web using video editing software such as the free programs iMovie for Apple Computers or Windows Movie Maker for PCs ➢ Save the movie into a web format such as .mov for QuickTime movies, or .wmv for Windows Media player and upload to Facebook using the file upload feature.

2. Mobile Devices to Facebook

You can get videos onto Facebook by recording them on mobile devices such as an iPhone or other cellphone.

To make it happen, you have to email your video, using your cellphone, to a dedicated email address (video@facebook.com). Facebook does not charge you for this cool service, but your cell provider might. If you are sending a long video to Facebook, the fees will really add up if your cell provider charges you by the minute to access the Web.

BEWARE OF JITTERY CELLPHONE VIDEOS

We've all seen videos taken by a cellphone that are jittery because the person couldn't hold their arm straight. Use your free hand to steady the elbow of the hand taking the video with your cellphone.

If you have a new phone and need to input the code Facebook sent you when you registered the phone number with it, just click on help near the middle of the Mobile Video Screen.

3. Webcam Video

If you are new to videos, it may seem complicated to get videos from your video camera to your computer and finally uploaded onto Facebook. It is not.

Here are the steps to getting video from your video camera onto your profile. Facebook will automatically recognize any video source. If you do not have a camcorder plugged into the USB port of your computer, it will recognize your Webcam.

RESPECT COPYRIGHTED MATERIAL

Videos uploaded on Facebook—even though the uploader agrees to release Facebook from any copyright violations and allow the video to be used and copied on Facebook—may be taken from outside of Facebook and still be under copyright. If the video is commercially produced yet uploaded by an individual who is not associated with the company who made the video, it is best to stay away from it.

It is easier to get videos from your Webcam to Facebook than from your camcorder to Facebook. If you have a Webcam already on your computer this is a quick video record and transfer process. Just point the Webcam in the right direction and click the button to begin. If your Webcam also has a microphone, Facebook will automatically recognize it so you can input sound. Regardless of how you get your video onto Facebook, all videos can be shared with friends . . . even if they are not your own. If you come across a good one, select the Share link next to it and send it to friends.

If you upload a video to your profile *anyone* who is in one of your networks can see the video and share it with friends. If you don't want the world seeing it, click the box that says "Show this video in my limited profile" when adding the video. Please visit the Privacy chapter of *Facebook Fanatic* to learn the various privacy settings for videos and also keep in mind that anyone who can view your videos can comment on them. You can even comment on your own videos if you feel the need!

4. HTML Box

Besides the HTML freedom Facebook gives you in various area like Notes to insert limited HTML codes, there is a little-know application that has been developed on the Facebook Platform specifically for HTML. It's much more powerful than normal Facebook HTML. In fact, using it will allow you show two videos on your profile at once! With it you can add a flash music playlist or video and even mp3 files. Where do you find this powerful elixir? Just follow this link and type "HTML Box" into the search window.

http://www.facebook.com/apps/?ref=wn

Choose your HTML Box privacy settings and add the application to your profile. Once you do, it's easy to place videos and music onto your profile. First know that Facebook does not allow <script> or <embed> HTML commands. So you can't just copy and paste the embedded video command from a YouTube video into the HTML Box. Instead, use the following format for videos in .SWF.

<fb:swf swfsrc="URL" height"###" width="380"/>

For videos in ShockWave Flash format, such as YouTube videos, use this code in the HTML Box.

<fb:flv src="URL" height="###" width="380"/>

ADD AN IMAGE TO VIDEOS

If you want to include an image along with the video showing in the HTML Box put the imgsrc tag before the final /. For instance, <fb:flv src="URL" height="###" width="380" imgsrc="IMAGE URL"/>.

5. Get myTV

The Facebook video player does not let you show YouTube videos directly and that creates a problem for some. Never fear. To skirt this conundrum get the myTV application.

Find this app here so can begin showing YouTube videos on your profile today: http://www.facebook.com/apps/application.php?api_key=7c1cdf5087d34bf3bcf72f05a7 d49545. What's more, you can search for top YouTube videos right from your profile. You can also import your favorites list right from YouTube. This powerful tool is free!

D. Facebook Diaries

Facebook has developed a video series of sorts where you can be the star of your own series. It is called Facebook Diaries and it is a great place to meet new friends and increase popularity.

Think of a cool theme and do a series of "diaries" and what the profile hits roll in. Facebook has teamed with the video site Ziddio to make it all happen. To get started, visit http://ziddio.com/facebook or search for Facebook Diaries within Facebook.

E. Make Money Off Facebook Videos

Did you know there a couple of great Websites that will let you upload Facebook videos and then will share a percentage of the revenue when a person clicks on an Internet ad showing next to the videos? If you have a popular video on Facebook, you are sitting on a digital moneymaking opportunity! People with popular videos have made thousands of dollars in click revenue off only one popular video. Listed below are the top video payment services and the amount of click revenue they will share with you.

Video Sharing Website	Click Revenue Sharing Percentage
Revver.com	50%
eeFoof.com	50%
Panjea.com	50%
Blip.tv	50%

LINK TO VIDEO REVENUE SITES

Since Facebook does not share click revenue with its users, you can upload your videos to one of the revenue sharing sites discussed above and provide the URL to it from your Facebook profile. This will drive even more traffic to those profiles and bring in more click revenue!

F. Video Comments

Videos, like Notes, are considered a public area of Facebook and therefore anyone can leave comments who can view your profile. When they do, their name is displayed and a link is provided to their profile. Not only that, but their default Facebook profile photo is also displayed. If you find a hot video on Facebook that is within one of your networks, leaving a comment of substance is a good way to get clicks and meet new friends.

60 Second Summary

Key Video Tips

- Anyone can comment on videos to gain popularity
- Use compelling words for your video title
- Videos are limited to 300 MB in size and must be under 15 minutes in length
- Add the HTML Box application to your profile to show YouTube videos on your profile using HTML codes
- Facebook Diaries are a great way to get popular and meet new friends
- A number of sites share click revenue with you for Facebook videos

What You'll Experience

Add Note Photos

Tag Friends in Notes

Email Note URL

Write Notes from Your Phone

Import a Blog into Notes

XIII   Notes

A. Notes Introduction

Notes are another great way to increase popularity on Facebook. Think of a Note as an online diary that is *very* public. On it you can publish your thoughts on just about anything.

☐ Notes

Notes are called Blogs most other places on the Internet. Yet there is some confusion regarding Blogs and their many different flavors. The word Blog is short for "Web Log". There are also Vlogs ("Video Logs") that contain short videos of people ranting about various subjects, as well as Podcasts ("iPod Broadcasts") that contain audio programs you can play on your computer. Facebook Notes are a combination of all of these. You can let the world know why you are an expert on your favorite band Snow Patrol, or how you learned to juggle on a unicycle. While you're at it, sprinkle in a few of your accomplishments for friends to peruse on a daily basis (or hourly if you have that much time on your hands). Be sure to add a few smilies while you're at it. Keep friends locked into what's happening in your world with Facebook Notes.

Videos are limited to 300 MB in size and must be under 15 minutes in length.

B. Create Notes

You can start a Note by clicking on "more" in the left-hand column of your profile and then selecting Notes. You will be presented with a page that contains the Notes of your friends. At the top of the screen you have three Note options, the first being My Notes.

Select "Write a New Note" from the screen that appears and you are ready to create your first Note. The title is limited to 65 characters and you have unlimited characters to use in the body of Notes.

Clicking to start a Note will launch an empty Note page that is ready for your comments and thoughts about the world in general. You can begin typing immediately. Once you post a Note entry both the title (usually the subject) and body are displayed on your profile instantly. Be careful since anyone browsing your profile can read your Note even if they are not your friend.

At the moment Facebook does not display your Note views. You cannot name a Facebook Note, add a skin, or change the background/text color at time of publication, but look for this to change in the future.

HTML looks great in the body of Notes, but it does not work, however, in the title.

C. Inserting HTML Into Notes

Spicing up Notes with HTML is a good way to draw the attention of friends who are unskilled in this area. To add zip, use these HTML codes.

Big Font

Make your font size large with this HTML: <big>Big Text Here</big>

Bold
Here is the HTML bold command: **Bold Text Here**

Bullet List
<ul>
<li>First Item in List<li>
<li>Second Item in List<li>
</ul>

Em-dash
This is how you create this kind of — dash: —

Heading
The text of each heading gets smaller as you add more of them in the body. Here is an example:

<h1>First Heading</h1>
<h2>Second Heading</h2>
<h3>Third Heading</h3>

Hyperlink
To add a hyperlink to Notes, just use this format:
<a href=http://www.bottletreebooks.com>BottleTree – The 'Net You Need to Know</a> or just type out http://www.bottletreebooks.com to provide the link only without the text.

USE THE HTTP://
If you want to type in a URL instead of using the href HTML code, you must include the http:// at the front of the URL. Just typing in www.bottletreebooks.com will not create an embedded link.

Indented
This is the indented text HTML code: <blockquote>Indented Text Here</blockquote>

Italics
To put text in italics use this HTML code: <i>*Italicized Text Here*</i>

Numbered List
<ol>
<li>First Item in List<li>
<li>Second Item in List<li>
</ol>

Small Font
Make your font size little with this HTML: <small>Small Text Here</small>

Strikethrough
To strikethrough text do this: <s>~~Strikethrough Text Here~~</s>

Subscript
This HTML is not listed on Facebook's site as an option, but it works just as well. To create a subscript do this: _{Subscript Text Goes Here}

INPUT SCIENTIFIC EQUATIONS
To write the symbol for water, type: H₂O. It will be displayed as H_2O on your profile.

Superscript
This HTML is also not listed on Facebook's site as an option, but it works. To create a subscript do this: ^{Superscript Text Goes Here}

INPUT MATHEMATICAL EQUATIONS
To write the symbol for energy, type E=MC² that will display as $E=MC^2$.

Underline

To underline text in HTML do this: <u>Underline Text Here</u>

HTML SPACES DO NOT MATTER... BUT USE THEM

Spaces do not matter between HTML tags and neither do returns that place tags on a separate line. Use both, however, to easily read what tags you are using and where they are in your HTML code.

D. Post a Note Comment

Facebook makes it easy to post a Note comment. Anyone reading your Note can leave a comment by clicking on the link of each post. Facebookers have 1000 characters in which to write a Note comment, which is the same amount of characters they have to write a Video comment. There is also no subject for a Note comment and standard HTML can be used just as it can when creating a new Note entry.

E. Changing Old Note Posts

Let's say two weeks after you posted an entry about what a troll your former boyfriend was, you've gotten back together. Quick, you have to change the old Note entry. Are you out of luck? No way. You can change a Note at any time by viewing it and then clicking on Edit. You can even remove an entry by clicking on Delete. Always be sure to run a spell check on the body of your Note before you post it to the world. You can simply copy and paste the text into any word processor and run spell check or type first in the word processor to check your spelling and grammar, and then copy and paste the text into the body of your Note. Be sure to view your Note entry afterwards just to ensure something is not screwed up and your HTML worked, etc

ORIGINAL POST DATE DOES NOT CHANGE

Is your friend claiming to have discovered a cool new band first by pointing to the date on his Note post? Don't be fooled. When a person edits their Note, the original post date does not change!

F. Import an Existing Blog

What if you already have a Blog established outside Facebook? Many people have been Blogging for years before signing up on Facebook and have built up a devout following on Blogger.com or BlogLines.com or BlogListings.com. Most of us find it hard to keep up one Blog, let alone two. That's why Facebook allows you to easily import an existing Blog. Click on "Import a Blog". On the page presented you will be asked to input a URL for a Website where your Blog resides or an Atom/RSS feed address. You must then check a box where you acknowledge you have rights to post the Blog. In other words, if you have rights, you can post third party Blogs that are not your own! Don't abuse the privilege. Displaying too many Blog posts in a day could get you blocked from posting by Facebook. Once your link to Notes is established, new Blog posts will automatically appear in Facebook. Over a period of time you can transition your readers over to Facebook.

If you don't want to import every post on your Blog, you can use URL links smartly. If you have built up a devout following on another Blog, keep your hard-earned readers by linking to certain Blog posts on Facebook Notes. For instance, let's say you have a science Blog somewhere on the Internet. You happen to post an article about a large grant your school received for a new science lab. If science posts won't fit into the theme of your Facebook profile because it is all about your school, just link to that particular post on your Blog because it is school related. Alternatively, you can always copy and paste a good post over to Notes. The choice is always yours on Facebook.

> Can imported Blogs be edited? No! An imported Blog cannot be changed once brought into Facebook. To edit it, you much change it on your Blog site.

Link to an Existing Blog Table 13.A
➢ Search for your Blog on the third party site and highlight the browser URL
➢ Right click and copy the URL address
➢ Paste the URL: <a href=http://INSERT URL HERE>Check out my Blog here!</a>
➢ Post your Facebook Note

G. Buzz Your Note

Notes are useless if no one reads them. A great way to jumpstart a new Note is through a little self-promotion. Your Facebook Note is simply a unique URL on the Internet just like your profile. You can display this link in emails and on a Website so that friends merely have to click on it to be taken to your Note.

1. Add Note URL to AOL IM Info Box

AOL Instant Messenger allows you to attach information to your screen name so that people you IM can read it even when you are not online. This is your AIM calling card and you can easily provide a hyperlink to your Facebook Note with it.

Hyperlink Facebook Note Via AIM Info Box Table 13.B
➤ Log into AIM → Select My AIM from the toolbar → Pick Edit Profile
➤ Click on Next until you reach the More Info screen
➤ Paste this HTML code into the window: <font face="Times New Roman" size="4">Read my Note<a href=PASTE FACEBOOK NOTE URL HERE target="_blank">My Facebook Note!</a></font>
➤ Click on Finish and you are all set

2. Add Note URL to Gmail Signatures

Link your Facebook Note automatically to Gmail messages using this HTML.

Add Facebook Note URL Hyperlink to Gmail Signatures Table 13.C
➤ Log into Gmail account → Pick Settings from top of page
➤ Paste this HTML code into the Signature box: Check out what I've got on Facebook at PASTE FACEBOOK NOTE URL HERE
➤ Click the radio button next to the Signature box
➤ Hit Save Changes at the bottom of the screen

3. Add Note URL to Hotmail Signatures

Link your Facebook Note automatically to Hotmail email messages using the following HTML.

Add Facebook Note URL Hyperlink to Hotmail Signatures **Table 13.D**
➤ Login to Hotmail account → Pick Options → Mail → Personal Signature ➤ Paste this HTML code into the box: Check out what I've got on Facebook at PASTE FACEBOOK NOTE URL HERE ➤ Click OK and you are all set

4. Add Note URL to Yahoo Mail Signatures

Link Facebook Notes automatically to Yahoo Mail messages with this HTML.

Add Facebook URL Hyperlink to Yahoo Mail Signatures **Table 13.E**
➤ Log into Yahoo Mail account ➤ Pick Options → Signature under Management column ➤ Paste this HTML code into the box: Check out my Facebook Note at [PASTE FACEBOOK NOTE URL HERE] ➤ Select box next to "Add signature to all outgoing messages" ➤ Click Save in the lower left corner

H. Add or Link to photos within Notes

When creating a Note you will see an image upload box under the body section. Browse your computer and then preview your Note *before* posting. Remember that photo size is limited to 4 MB. You can also tag friends in Notes. This is not their photos, however, that we're talking about. When you place their name in a Note just type in their name again in the "Tag people in this note" box. A link will be created to that person's profile. Let's say you want to include an image from the Web or one you've taken with your digital camera and put it on your Note. A great way to link to it is to insert the URL where the cool photo is found on the Web.

Add Note Photo URL **Table 13.F**
➤ Locate the photo on the Web and right click on it ➤ Select Properties to view URL of the photo → ➤ Highlight URL and right click on it → Select copy (URL ends in .jpg or .gif) ➤ Paste the URL: <a href=http://INSERT URL HERE>Check out this surfing photo here!</a> → Post Note

I. Add videos to Notes

Posting a link to a video on Notes sounds difficult, but it's really easy and will set your Notes apart from thousands of other Notes on Facebook. All you have to do is insert the video URL code into your Note. Below shows how to do this for Facebook, AOL, Yahoo, YouTube, and Google Video.

1. Add Facebook Video Links

Getting funny or cool videos from within Facebook on your Note is easy.

Link to Facebook Videos on Notes Table 13.G
➢ Find a video on Facebook → Right click the URL in the browser window ➢ Select Copy → Open a new Note ➢ Paste the URL: <a href=http://INSERT URL HERE>Watch this cool video!</a> → Post Note

2. Add YouTube Video Links

Google's YouTube is the leader in Internet videos and you will find some of the best videos in this space.

Link to YouTube Videos on Notes Table 13.H
➢ Find a video on YouTube.com → Next to it is the About This Video block.

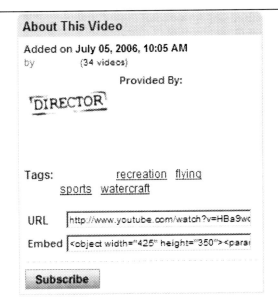

> ➤ Click anywhere in the URL rectangle then select Copy by right clicking
> ➤ Open a new Note
> ➤ Paste the URL: <a href=http://INSERT URL HERE>Check out this video!</a> → Post Note

3. Add Google Video Links

Google's search technology powers its video engine. Use it to easily find great videos to display on your Note. Once you have added the video URL to Notes, users can click on it to view it.

Link to Google Videos on Notes Table 13.I
➤ Find a video at www.video.google.com ➤ Right click on the URL in the browser window → Select Copy ➤ Open a new Note ➤ Paste the URL: <a href=http://INSERT URL HERE>Check out this video!</a> → Post Note

4. Add Yahoo Video Links

Yahoo is an Internet portal wrapped in media of all kinds. Videos are a natural extension of Yahoo's media emphasis. Here is how to get them onto your Note.

Link to Yahoo Videos on Notes Table 13.J
➤ Find a video at www.video.yahoo.com
➤ Right click on the URL in the browser window → Select Copy
➤ Open a new Note
➤ Paste the URL: <a href=http://INSERT URL HERE>Watch this video!</a>
➤ Post Note

You do not have to set up an account with AOL, YouTube, Google or Yahoo to view their videos. You can access at will and remain somewhat anonymous.

5. Add AOL Video Links
America Online (AOL) has quickly developed one of the best video sites on the Internet. Link to its videos on Notes.

Link to AOL Videos on Notes Table 13.K
➤ Find a video at www.video.aol.com
➤ Right click on the URL in the browser window → Select Copy
➤ Open a new Note
➤ Paste the URL: <a href=http://INSERT URL HERE>Check out this video!</a> → Post Note

J. Publish Free Articles
The key to any successful Note is to keep traffic flowing . . . not just with new users, but also with repeat users. Content on a Note is like food, you can have the best in the world but if visitors to your Note restaurant always have to eat leftovers, they are going to stop visiting. Internet users want fresh, hot content that is tasty. That's why Notes are so successful when done right. The information is constantly updated and is interesting. So keep your content fresh, hot and tasty to get return users. A great way to add relevant content to a Note is to publish *free* articles available on the Web. There are thousands of Web articles available for free on the Internet. Simply conduct a search on the terms "free articles" and "free content articles" to pull up a listing of sites.

Top Free Content Sites Table 13.L
➤ ContentDesk.com   ➤ EzineArticles.com   ➤ FindSticky.com   ➤ IdeaMarketers.com   ➤ isnare.com   ➤ GoArticles.com

K. Create a Note Text Banner

Since both your Note title and body are shown on your profile, you can make your own text banner. What's a text banner? Check out this Poe banner.

```
PPPPPPP
P       P
PPPPPPP
P
P
P
            OOOOOOOO
            O           O
            O           O
            O           O
            O           O
            OOOOOOOO
                        EEEEEEE
                        E
                        E
                        EEEEEEE
                        E
                        E
                        EEEEEEE
```

If you love Edgar Allan Poe (and who doesn't) a banner like this will let the world know. The Note segment of your profile is the best place to create a banner like this.

L. Send Notes from Your Phone

There are two ways to get Notes from your cellphone onto Facebook. Both fall under the Facebook Mobile application.

The key email address you must remember for Mobile Notes is: notes@facebook.com. You can email text or html from your phone into Notes; but first, you must sign up. When you first sign up for Facebook Mobile service, Facebook will send you a unique code after they get your email. You must then enter your code on the site.

Test your cellphone by your computer and input the one-time code so that you will have no trouble from the road

Once the correct code is inputted, you are all set and do not have to enter another one. Apart from emailing text to Notes, you can also send SMS to Notes. Here is a sample text command to send a Note about a Website: "Note Check Out http://www.bottletreebooks.com".

USE HTML FROM YOUR PHONE
Anything following the Note command will be inserted into Notes. This creates an automatic link. Take this example: Note <a href=http://INSERT URL HERE>Cool Website!</a>

M. Notes About You
Facebook also lets you quickly learn which friends have tagged you in their Notes. This is the "Notes about you" portion. The link is provided at the top of your main Notes page.

Keep in mind that only friends can tag you in Notes. If they are not your direct friend they will not be able to tag you even if they know who you are.

N. Visit Popular Notes
Want to see the hottest Notes on the Facebook planet? Click on the link titled "Popular Notes" at the top of your main Notes page.

My Notes | Notes about You | Popular Notes

If you want your Notes to become popular and get tons of comments, be sure to ask a question in the title. For instance, "Should I leave?" or "Are the Tigers the best team?" or "Is 'Catcher in the Rye' the best novel of the past 100 years?" Notes are a great way to post quizzes and polls. If your Notes become very popular, your friends will zoom.

Visit the privacy Chapter of *Facebook Fanatic* to ensure you secure Notes on your profile to your comfort level.

60 Second Summary

Key Note Tips
• HTML is not allowed in the title
• Facebook does not display the number of Note views you have had
• Provide the URL to your Notes outside of Facebook
• Post date and time does not change when you edit a Note
• Publish free articles in Notes from free content sites
• Create a Note text banner to grab attention

What You'll Experience

Swapping on Marketplace

Selling Tips

Marketplace Privacy

Why Photos Are Key

XIV   Marketplace

A. Marketplace Introduction

Marketplace is *the* place on the Internet to list just about anything you have to sell to Facebook's 30 million users. What great exposure! Did we mention it's all free? That's right, there isn't even a listing fee and Facebook does not get a percentage of the sales price for that old TV you are trying to get rid of. With the tips below you will learn how to make Marketplace *your* place on Facebook.

On the flip side, there is also no charge for buying stuff at Facebook Marketplace, but the number of ads you see may be limited. Only those within one of your networks can view your Marketplace listing unless the listing is designated for all networks.

MARKETPLACE PRIVACY

Understand that anyone who can view your marketplace listing can send you a message about purchasing it. On the buyer's side, any questions you ask the seller can be incorporated into the listing along with the answer.

B. Categories

To get started, click More in the left-hand column of your profile and you will be presented with the Marketplace link. Select it and you are automatically taken to the overall Marketplace page within your networks.

There you will see general listings for all items being sold. The items are displayed on the page from newest to oldest, which usually means that items listed on the day you are searching are shown at the top of the screen. Old listings are shown at the bottom of all active listings. Sponsored Listings are displayed in the right-hand column.

SELLING TIPS

If you are selling a big ticket item like a car, motorcycle or boat, opt for a sponsored listing and be sure to include *all* Facebook networks instead of just the ones to which you belong.

When selling items on Facebook Marketplace you have six subcategories from which to choose. Under housing you have four subcategories and you can also post jobs and free stuff. Why would you ever want to list free stuff? You may want to find a good home for an animal or can't bear to throw your beat-up copy of "Sense and Sensibility" in the trash. There is even a dedicated category for Free Stuff. Here are the possibilities.

Category/Subcategory	Category/Subcategory
For Sale	**Housing**
For Sale ➢ Books ➢ Cars ➢ Electronics ➢ Furniture ➢ Other ➢ Tickets	Housing ➢ Real Estate ➢ Rentals/Apartments ➢ Other ➢ Sublets
Other	**Jobs**
Other ➢ Found Items ➢ Everything Else	Jobs (too many to list here)
Free Stuff	
Free Stuff	

Next we'll take a look at the want ad categories. Before you post an item for sale, ensure that someone is not looking for that item in the want ads. If they are, you will be saved a lot of time and effort. Sometimes, they may be willing to pay more than you had anticipated selling the item for in the first place.

Category	Category
Housing Wanted	Item Wanted
Looking for Work	Other Wanted

C. My Listings

Facebook provides an easy way for you to view all of your Marketplace listings in one place. Just select My Listings from the top of the page.

A good way to check how much interest an item is getting, besides inquiry messages, is the number of item views. Once an item sells you can remove a listing on this page and can also add new listings at any time. It's also good practice to remove an item that has been for sale for over 30 days and relist it as a new item. Not only will your new (old) item be shown on the main Marketplace page, but it will also generate more buzz as a newly listed item.

GOOD PHOTOS ARE A MUST
If your items isn't getting any page views and you have priced it right, it's likely because of your photo. Take a better one and watch the page views increase.

D. My Friends' Listings

A neat feature Facebook has developed is where it lets you see your friends' Marketplace listings at the click of a mouse button. At the top of the Marketplace page you will see this link.

Marketplace   My Listings   **My Friends' Listings**   Add a new listing

Swapping works great on Facebook. If a friend wants an item you have for sale, check to see if they have listed an item on your wish list. If that is the case, offer to swap. Each person pays his or her own shipping costs. Get creative on Marketplace. You have nothing to lose and only friends to gain.

E. Listing Items

Creating a listing in Marketplace is not hard. Facebook provides a useful form that you fill out. Click on "Add a New Listing" at anytime within Marketplace and you are on your way.

Marketplace > Listing

Facebook gives you unlimited characters to use as the title for your listing, which is required. It is best, however, to keep your title short and to the point. Likewise, in the required description of the item, you are given unlimited characters in which to describe what you are selling. This is the area where you do not want to skimp. You must sell your item (the sizzle more than the steak) and give at least enough description to let potential buyers make an informed decision. If they have to work hard by sending you multiple messages, they may not bother.

DON'T SKIMP ON THE DESCRIPTION
If your description is better than an identical item being sold by someone else, you will likely get the sale if quality and price are equal.

Below the description is a box where you choose whether the item is New or Used, with the default being the latter. You can next input the price (in US dollars) for which you are willing to sell the item. Do not inflate the price. Most people on Facebook are not looking to barter the price down so make it realistic.

Under the price you can check a box to add the listing to your profile. Generally this is a good idea especially if the item you are selling is related to the theme of your profile. For example, if you have a Star Wars theme and you are selling your collection of 1980 Empire Strikes Back cards, ensure it is listed on your profile since friends and visitors will be interested in the subject. When you list your items you have the option of picking any of your networks in which to list your items. You can even select to have the item shown outside of these networks. Be sure to review the privacy chapter of *Facebook Fanatic* to protect yourself on Facebook Marketplace.

Finally, you can add photos to your Marketplace listing. Apart from your description, the photo of the item is the second most important section of your listing. It is what will bring potential buyers into your door and the description will hopefully get them to buy. Remember that photo sizes are limited to 4 MB on Facebook.

ADD MULTIPLE PHOTOS
Take multiple photos of your item from different angles. This will give perspective buyers a quick feel for the quality of the item. If you are selling a book, be sure to take photos of the front, back, spine and the copyright page. There are collectors out there looking for first editions.

60 Second Summary

Key Marketplace Tips

- Marketplace listings are totally free
- When purchasing an item on Marketplace, any questions will be displayed
- Never divulge more than you are willing to give out on your profile
- For best results upload multiple photos
- You can give stuff away on Marketplace like pets, etc.
- Swap stuff on Marketplace if another has an item that you want

What You'll Experience

Most Advertised Genres

Popular Groups

Make Money Off Facebook Videos & Song Downloads

Get Your Songs on iTunes

XV   Buzz a Band

If you are an undiscovered/unsigned band, it is crucial to get the attention you need and Facebook is one of the places to do it. At your fingertips is a potential audience of over 30 million registered users! Do you want to become a digital rock star on Facebook? Do you want a crazy number of friends from all over the planet who will worship your band? Have you ever wanted the power to sign with the label of your choosing? Do you want to turn grassroots popularity into hard cash? If *yes*, sit back, strap yourself in and get ready to explode your band's popularity on Facebook with these tips and tricks to buzz your band.

1. Pick a Great Screen Name

Having a screen name that is easy to remember on Facebook is important for your band's popularity and success. Since you are limited to your real first name and your last name, or first letter or your last name, it is important for the front man or woman of your band to get their name out there. Sign up quickly to register your name before an unofficial group or groupie takes it. If you are forced to pick a less desirable screen name, do not worry. Facebook lets you change your screen name at any time.

2. Get Friends and More Friends

Facebook popularity, just like real life, is centered on how many friends you have. To get a ton of friends—we're talking hundreds—you cannot just sit back and wait for them to come beat a path to your Facebook digital door. Remember this magic Facebook formula:

> **Friends = Groupies => Even More Groupies**

People become your friend on Facebook because they like your music. When they have made this fan-status leap of faith, they will work to get you even more fans. That is the beauty of Facebook when trying to quickly build your fan base. People love to show off that they have discovered an awesome band on Facebook. But this does not come overnight. Accept *all* the friend requests you get to start this pile growing. As it does, so will your band's popularity. Last, be sure to put the members of your band in your top friend spots so they will also get visits to their profile.

3. Most Popular Genres

Some types of music get more free advertising on Facebook than others. Like any good marketer, you need to get a presence in these areas to attract attention. If your music can fit in a number of different categories, pick the one that is most popular. For example, if your music can be either Black Metal or just Metal, pick the later category to broaden your potential listeners and list your genre at the top of your interest sections.

4. Theme Profile Photo

You are an up and coming band. Show it in your profile photos. Fans want to see you up on stage, playing and singing. That's why your profile photo should reflect the theme of your band. Fans want to believe in their bands and their lifestyle. If you are a death metal band, don't show that vacation photo of you in a Hawaiian shirt.

THIS INCLUDES ACTIVITIES & INTERESTS

The Activities and Interest areas of your profile are a great place to further build the theme of your band and tell about the gigs you've been playing. You have unlimited words to use for this purpose.

Tip

5. Add Facebook URL to Email Messages

Your Facebook URL can easily be added to outgoing email messages in the form of a hyperlink that your non-Facebook fans can click on to be taken to your profile. If Facebook is your only Web presence, it's important to build up friends and fans on your profile. Below is an example with everything from the http to just before the first > being the Facebook profile URL.

```
Put a link to your Facebook profile on AIM:
<a href=http://www.facebook.com/p/Andy_B/527300036>Facebook me!</a>
```

Visit the URL chapter of *Facebook Fanatic* to learn how to add this link into the messages of the Web's most popular email engines.

6. Add Great Band Quotes

The Favorite Quotes area of your interest section is important for bands though it may not seem that way at first. Here is where you show what authors, politicians, or religious figures inspire you the most. Fans like to see what makes their bands tick. So pay adequate attention to this area. Of course, you can even quote yourself or another band! Two of the best (and free) quotes sites on the Internet are wisdomquotes.com and quoteland.com.

7. Get Popular Friends

There is an old proverb that says they who want friends must make themselves friendly, or something like that. The same applies to Facebook. Stop hiding within the confines of your profile and get out there and try to *make* new friends. A great place to start is with popular Facebookers in your networks. Do not forget about non-movie/TV celebrities like sports stars (for some reason there is a lot of big-time wrestling stars on Facebook), authors, and comedians.

REMEMBER "THANKS" COMMENTS
If you get a famous friend, be sure to post a "Thanks for the Add" comment to get even more exposure at the popular profile.

8. List Favorite Books

At first it may appear that the Favorite Books area on your profile is the least exciting and important for a band. This is not the case. Here is where you let fans know what books impressed you and made you the songwriter you are today. Provide URL links to your favorite books on Amazon.com. To do this, visit the book on Amazon then copy and paste the URL in your browser window into the Favorite Books section. Tell fans to do the same, just the opposite, by copying and pasting it into their browser window to visit the page and buy the book.

9. Favorite Music is a Must

The interest section that is a no brainer for band members is the Favorite Music section. Most of us can go on for days about the music we like. This section gives you that chance in spades with unlimited words. Of course list your own music here, but if your style is like other music, tell fans. But more importantly, tell them why you like the songs you have chosen. Favorite bands or albums? List them here.

10. Update Gigs From the Road

If you are playing anywhere on the road (since Facebook reaches the world), broadcast the dates on your profile so fans new and old can see you play. Create a quiz to show where you are playing next or write on your own Wall or post in Notes. Be creative.

With the Web portion of Facebook Mobile you can stay in touch with fans on the road. The graphics are sparse, but the meat of the matter is there for *all* sections of your profile. Mobile Web is where you can surf your Facebook profile at will. Always be connected! Did we mention that you can also stay in touch with the Events portion of Facebook? This is essential when on the road and you want to book impromptu gigs.

11. Add Photos and Notes on the Road

If you have some great pictures from last night's gig, you can easily zap them to your Facebook profile by using Mobile Uploads. It is the coolest and quickest way to get info onto your Facebook profile when traveling. Want to send a blurb to Notes about the concert while you are at it? No problem. On Facebook it's easy.

After your cellphone is enabled on Facebook, use these two email addresses: photos@facebooks.com and notes@facebook.com to upload photos and Notes, respectively.

12. SMS on the Road

Okay, so you can upload photos, update Events and send Notes on the road. Great. You can also SMS your fans using the handy commands below with Facebook SMS.

You can conduct your Facebook business by texting to FBOOK, which are the numbers 32665. Keep in mind that you can always text fans on Facebook even if they don't have a cellphone since your messages go right to their Facebook profile.

Action	Command	Example Text
Add a Friend	Add	Add Bob Marks
Fire a Friend	Fire	Fire Bob Marks
Get Cell Number	Cell	Cell Bob Marks
Message	Msg	Msg Bob Marks Are You Ready
Poke	Poke	Poke Bob Marks
Search Profile	N/A	Bob Marks
Wall Post	Wall	Wall Bob Marks Ace Your Exam
Write a Note	Note	Note Bob Marks Check Out www.TaleSale.com

13. Got Skype? Forward Calls to Cellphone

When your band is on the road, make sure you do not miss a call. All you have to do is forward them to your cellphone. Your mobile Skype settings are key to keeping up with Facebook when traveling and you do not have Internet access.

Steps to Forward Skype Calls Table 15.A
➤ Login to Skype → Click Tools → Select Options → Click Call Forwarding ➤ Check the box next to "Forward calls when I'm not on Skype"

YOU ARE CHARGED FOR THIS SERVICE

While Skype to Skype calls are free to anyone in the world at anytime, forwarding your Skype calls to a cellphone requires payment to your Skype account. You must fund this account before receiving forwarded calls.

14. Upload, Upload, Upload

Got 10, 20, 30 or even more songs? Make sure you upload them to your profile on Facebook. Search for the Facebook Jukebox application and get uploading today by adding your own songs to Facebook.

15. Sell Band Photos

Viral marketing is spreading on Facebook. A great way to get in on the game is to sell photo items from QOOP. Never heard of it? Well, Facebook has teamed with QOOP (www.QOOP.com), one of the Internet's leading photo printing services. With QOOP you can order photos, posters, etc. You name it and QOOP can usually print your photos on it. Get creative and sell band items in many different ways on your Website, eBay or Facebook Marketplace.

16. Take a Page from Blake

What is Blake? Never heard of the band. Well you soon will. Blake is a boyband with a common background in classical music that got together on Facebook and also found a manager on Facebook. The band derives their name from 18th Century poet William Blake. When the band found that Daniel Glatman, who formerly managed another boyband, was in their network they began trying to make contact with him. He responded and signed on as Blake's manager. As reported by *Metro*, Daniel Glatman negotiated a £1million, five-album record deal for them. Maybe you will be as fortunate!

17. Be a Note Hog

Notes are vital to making your profile "sticky" and for ensuring your band stays in the minds of listeners when tons of other bands are trying to muscle you out. If you are playing gigs on the road, get a laptop with wireless Internet access so you can stay in touch with fans. Note every day or multiple times a day, letting them know when and where you will be playing. Fans love to read your experiences on the road!

INCLUDE SET DETAILS
Do not forget to provide a list of the music you played in your set, what you were wearing, fans in attendance, how many instruments the band wrecked, etc.

18. Post a Contest

A great way to get fans reading your Note is to have periodic contests. How do you have one? Easy. State on your profile that you will be having a Note contest in the next few weeks. On the day you decide, post a trivia question about the band or one of your songs or tour date venues, etc on Notes. The first one to answer the question correctly by leaving a comment gets an autographed T-shirt or CD.

19. Enable the SnapVine.com Widget

By placing the SnapVine.com widget on your profile groupies can leave the band personal voice messages. Post the best ones on your Note for everybody to read. Search the Web for "Facebook Snapvine" to find reviews on the app and the app itself.

20. Link, Link, Link

To get as much traffic as possible, you have to send out email messages that include hyperlinks to your profile. You can also provide direct links to your Notes. Visit the URL section of *Facebook Fanatic* to learn how to *automatically* add a link to your profile from AOL, Hotmail, Gmail, and Yahoo Mail.

LINK TO YOUR WEBSITE
Provide a link on your Facebook profile to your band's Website. Also link back from your Website to your profile. Get traffic flowing both ways.

21. Make a Video

Some of the coolest videos are homemade and have a documentary feel to them. Many are shot in black and white. The jittery, unprofessional look is in style. You certainly do not need an expensive video camera for this. Use one lying around the apartment. Not sure how to post your video? Visit the video section of *Facebook Fanatic* to find out how.

What is key to getting your shorts on mobile devices such as a cellphone or video iPod is to convert your video files into the correct format. Cellphones play video in 3GP format. For PCs Xilisoft has published its 3GP Converter at xilisoft.com for downloading. Keep the file size as small as possible to limit download time on mobile devices.

> Apple requires all films and shorts to be sized in a 640x480 format to play on video iPods.

For video iPods there is a special iPod format. You can download MoviePod at nullriver.com in formats that work for the PC or Mac. The file can be of any size. When you produce a video in the video iPod format you open your potential audience up to the tens of millions of video iPod owners.

> At ffmpegx.com you can download free cellphone conversion software for the Mac.

22. Get a Filmmaker to Make Your Video

If your band is looking to make its first video, contact an upstart filmmaker on Facebook to do it for you. Why would they want to spend their time making a free video? If you are a hot band, making a great video can launch an unknown filmmaker into the lucrative video business. How will you find filmmakers on Facebook? Well, there are a number of ways to go about it. First, conduct a filmmaker search. This will pull up all types of filmmakers in every imaginable genre. A second, and more direct way to go about your search is to search for a filmmaker at your school or college. If you cannot find any recent music video posts, post a new topic by clicking in the upper right-hand corner and ask other alumni if they know of any.

ATTEND FILM FESTIVALS

Check out upstart filmmakers at local festivals. If you live in a small city that doesn't have film festivals, try to attend one when traveling or playing gigs out of state.

23. Post Your Music Video

A sweet video is one of the best ways to vault your band's popularity. If you have one, post it on your profile and Facebook Video. You should also post it on YouTube, AOL Video and Yahoo Video. Visit the video section of *Facebook Fanatic* to learn how to get a video from your camera or hard drive onto Facebook.

24. Post a Music Related Video

If you do not have a video of your band, post a video that is music related. For instance, if you toured the Gibson guitar factory in Memphis and then picked out your guitar afterwards, post this video so fans can see what cool strings you have.

POST A VIDEO FROM YOUTUBE

Is there a sweet video on YouTube that shows how your amps or instruments are made? If you don't have a music video of your band, show one of these videos by inserting the video URL from YouTube.

25. Leave a Comment with URL

Did Mom ever tell you to keep comments to yourself? Well, Facebook is not the place to follow Mom's instructions . . . if you want to become popular. Once you become friends with a well-trafficked profile or popular friend, send a comment over to keep your photo in the front and center. This includes authors, books, films, Notes, and groups.

REMEMBER "THANKS" COMMENTS

If you get a new fan/friend, be sure to post a "Thanks for the Add" comment on The Wall of their profile to get even more exposure. Poke them once in a while, too.

You have to get out there and cast your photo/comments net in as many popular places as possible to catch the most friends. If you are casting your net in shallow waters by making a few friend requests a day, you're not going to catch big fish. A great way to catch that digital mackerel is to become friends with featured profiles such as Facebook Diaries.

26. Attach Video to Email Messages

It sounds complicated, but it is easy to attach your band's music videos or video interviews to email messages. Just copy the video URL shown in the browser URL window and email or IM that link to your friends. Since it is a hyperlink, all they have to do is click on it to be taken to the Facebook profile where the video is showing.

27. A Day in the Life

If you want to do a video that is between a music video and a movie, film a day in the life of your band and post it on Facebook. Watch The Beatles's "A Hard Day's Night" to see how they did it back in the day. Post the video on Facebook Diaries and watch your fans increase.

28. Write a Movie Soundtrack

If you can get just one song on a popular movie soundtrack, this will pave the way to success for your band. Better yet, try to do songs for the entire soundtrack of a movie. If you are a fledgling band, try hooking up with a relatively new filmmaker on Facebook and offer to write songs for an indie movie. It is a great way to help each other out and to cross-pollinate your fan bases.

All American Rejects scored the entire soundtrack for the movie John Tucker Must Die.

29. Create a Playlist

Did you know that the individual members of your band can create a playlist of your band's songs? The more Facebookers that place songs from it onto their profile, the more your playlist will rise in the rankings. You can even mix your songs in among more popular band songs. Search for the Facebook Jukebox application and get started.

30. Post Lyrics

Fans love to read the lyrics of your songs. Post them exclusively on The Wall or in Notes to keep fans coming back for more. Teach them what they need to get their information directly from the source. When you are playing gigs on the road, you will be surprised how many fans on the front row can sing along word for word with your songs. This is fan loyalty at its best.

31. Conduct a Video Interview

The only thing better for fans than being able to hear your music is for them to hear how it came into being. Gather your band around a pool table or in your favorite coffee house or in front of your instruments, and record a video interview. Remember to look in the camera when talking (unless you're being super cool). If you have glasses do not sit close to your computer monitor or turn it off to eliminate glare.

A LITTLE PLANNING IS GOOD

Get interview questions laid out beforehand and think of what you are going to say so the video does not have to be cropped. Do not rehearse or you will sound canned and boring.

After recording your interview, upload it to Facebook and show it on your profile.

32. List the Band's Bio

Have music experience? Did you win first prize in a band competition? Have you opened for a popular act? You have unlimited characters to use in the About section of your profile. Do not be shy. This is a great place to give your bio as a band.

33. Conduct a Poll

Polls are a good way to focus the attention of Facebook readers on a particular topic for your band or album. The best polls have one question and contain between 2 and 5 possible answers. Notes is a great place to conduct a poll or you can simply leave the question on The Wall for comments.

MUSIC POLL

Do a poll about your music. This is a good way to generate fan base interaction and to gage what they would like to see more of in the future.

Here are some other good poll ideas. Most are general in nature, but will make your profile sticky.

Great Poll Ideas Table 15.B
➢ Trivia about your favorite band, movie, TV show, sports team, book, etc.
➢ Who is the best athlete?
➢ What is your dream car?
➢ What do you fear the most?
➢ Questions about the best city or place to go on vacation
➢ Which amusement park has the best rollercoasters?
➢ Best pickup line
➢ Worst pickup line
➢ Who will win a sporting event or election?
➢ Best chick flick
➢ Best book of the last 100 years (Hint: *Catcher in the Rye*)
➢ Prime location to get a tattoo
➢ Coolest tattoo

34. Post Guitar Tabs

Lots of music fans are into playing instruments themselves. A good feature for your Facebook profile is to provide guitar tabs in interest sections of your profile. If you already have tabs displayed on your Website, you can copy and paste them into Facebook or link to your guitar tab's page by providing the URL.

35. Show Your Cover Image

If you album is not widely available, scan in a cover of your CD and get it on your profile. Instead of showing your face as the default profile picture, show your album's cover. This is a great way to make your photo stand apart from the thousands of faces on Facebook.

36. Sell Band Posters

Check out AllPosters.com, which sells band and movie posters. Right now the site focuses on major bands like U2 and the Stones, but you may be able to get a poster of your band on sale too.

37. Compile an Electronic Press Kit

Without leaving their wingback leather chairs with inlaid studs, music producers can check you out. That is the beauty of Facebook. You no longer need huge press kits filled with pictures, CDs, and descriptions; and you no longer have to physically print and mail a press kit when you can have a much better (and less expensive) one on your profile.

Key Items for a Digital Press Kit on Facebook Table 15.C
➢ Biography; Photos; Lots of Groupies; Lyrics; Tour dates, places and times ➢ Music; Videos

38. Get Signed With a Label

Getting signed with a label is easier said than done. There are simply no A-B-C steps to follow. Never fear. Facebook and what it is doing for bands is huge. We saw above that the band Blake got signed with a label after finding its manager on Facebook. To get started, recognize your profile as your calling card to getting popular and recognized on Facebook. If it is unprofessional, no labels will come calling. There is simply too much competition. Once you have a great profile with a digital press kit, search for managers on the Web and email them a hyperlink so they can click over to your profile.

CHECK OUT BANDS WITH A SIMILAR SOUND

If you find a band on Facebook with a similar sound and they have already signed with a label, find out which one from their profile or CD insert. Then, approach a competitive label and market why your band is better. This is guerrilla band marketing at its finest.

39. Merchandise With BandMerch

Are you a new or established band that wants to start selling t-shirts, coffee mugs, belt buckles, etc? No matter how big or small your band is, BandMerch can offer you a solution that is both high-quality, and cost-effective. With BandMerch you can work to design your logo and list different items you wish to sell. It is all done over the Web and you do not have to carry any inventory! Lugging around boxes of T-shirts is tough when living out of a van doing gigs on the road. To contact BandMerch, shoot an email to Product@BandMerch.com. You can also visit its Website to see stuff from other bands at: bandmerch.com. When you start selling on BandMerch, be sure to link to the site on your Facebook profile.

40. Enter the Billboard 100 Without a Label

The Wall Street Journal reports that members of the band Lustra used a great strategy to get on the Billboard 100 list. First, they got a huge following on a social networking site by marketing themselves. They then asked their fans to continuously contact iTunes to carry their single "Scotty Doesn't Know". Apple finally gave in and the song got listed on iTunes. It got so many downloads that it entered the Billboard Pop 100 at No. 59. The unbelievable thing is that Lustra does not have a label and received no radio play. Along the lines of what Lustra did, if your band does not have downloadable songs on iTunes, get Facebook fans to email Apple. Eventually Apple will get the hint that there is a market for your songs on iTunes. Who knows, your band's song may even be offered as the iTunes download of the week. Bands: It can be done and the tips and tricks in *Facebook Fanatic* can get you there.

41. Post iTunes Link Maker on Facebook Profile

What is iTunes Link Maker? It is a dedicated Apple connection that lets you link directly to your band's song (or any song for that matter) on iTunes so fans can pay to download it.

Once you get a song on iTunes link to it from your Facebook profile. Follow this link to get iTunes Link Maker today and remember to incorporate the link on your profile: http://phobos.apple.com/WebObjects/MZSearch.woa/wa/itmsLinkMaker.

42. Use iTunes Producer
iTunes Producer is a free Apple utility that allows you to convert songs from almost any digital format to ACC, Apple's dedicated digital song recording format.

You will need to have songs converted to ACC in order for them to be downloadable on iTunes. So, after Facebook fans clamor for your band's songs to be included on iTunes, convert them to ACC (your songs not your fans) and you will be set to launch. To get iTunes Producer you must sign up for iTunes Label Connect at: http://www.apple.com/itunes/musicmarketing/ and then follow the instructions to download.

43. Conduct an Interview
We've learned that Notes are vital to making your profile "sticky" and for ensuring your writing stays in the minds of readers when lots of other bands are trying to muscle you out. A good way to pique fan interest and get them reading Notes is to conduct an interview in question-and-answer fashion.

44. Post a Music Related Video
If at the moment you do not have a video, post one that is music related. There are some great ones on YouTube. All you have to do is search on the tags such as guitars, drums, amps, etc. Read the video chapter of *Facebook Fanatic* to learn how multiple videos can be placed on your profile.

45. Show Off Your Fans
Just like profile views and song plays, the number of fans/groupies your band has is very important. Tons of groupies along with great music can get you signed with a label. Do not be afraid to tout the number of fans you have.

46. Hyperlink Your Way to Success
Hyperlinking is the best way to get fans from your Facebook profile to your band's Website. A copy and paste of the URL into any Internet browser and they are there.

While you are at it, ensure you hyperlink back from your Website to your Facebook profile. You can make your own "Share on Facebook" HTML link to put on your Website. This makes it easy for visitors to click it and share the content on Facebook with their friends. Fine. But if you really want to make HTML links come alive, there are special HTML meta tags that you must insert to preview the content. See the Posted Items chapter of *Facebook Fanatic* for linking options. The minor problem with sharing content using these links is that they only provide a link and little else. There are no meta tags that tell Facebook what type of content it is (audio, video, image, text, etc.). Add the following basic tags to ensure the title of your song and a short description are imported into Facebook. This also includes the initial image of your content, if it is an image or video, which is displayed on Facebook.

Meta Tags
<meta name="title" content="'AdSense Unleashed' book published by BottleTree" />
<meta name="description" content="Learn the tips you need to make money by showing free Google ads on your Website." />
<link rel="image_src" href="http://www.bottletreebooks.com/AdsenseUnleashed.jpg" />

Basic Content Tags
An example short story could have the following:
<meta name="title" content="The Legend of Sleepy Hollow" />
<meta name="description" content="Icabod Crain and the Headless Horseman. Need we say more?" />
<link rel="image_src" href="URLofCOVERIMAGE.jpg" />

The title and summary tags are the minimum requirements for any preview, so be sure to include these two.

As shown, title contains the preview title, description contains the preview summary and image_src contains the preview image.

Type of Content Tag
You may specify the type of content being shared by using the following tag:
<meta name="medium" content="medium_type" />
Valid values for *medium_type* are "audio", "image", "video", "news", "Note" and "mult".

* To make your videos embeddable on Facebook, send a request to developers-help@facebook.com. This request should include the domain names of the values you

will use for the video source URL (in the video_src link tag above). You must do this to ensure your videos play correctly.

47. Start a Group About Your Band

Facebook groups are a fantastic way to get your band noticed. If you don't have one started already, ask fans to start a group about your band. If your band gets a fan club group, post comments in it regularly! Fans will love this. You should also post comments on profiles that have playlists of one of your songs. If one of your band members attended a school or college on Facebook, this is a good place to get known.

48. Become a Member of a Group

Even if you do have a group dedicated to your band, it is always good to post in a music-related group for your school or college just to keep your name out there. Search for your genre of music on Facebook and you will be surprised at the number of groups out there.

49. Start a Topic in a Group

Start a fun topic within a popular music-related group. As the creator of the thread, your band's photo and link to your profile will always be shown.

50. Circulate a Digital Flyer

We've all seen how magazines and national newspapers get plastered with the latest offerings by big name bands. Now, even if you are a new band, you can do the same thing, but digitally, and reach the entire Facebook world. All it takes is for you to post an image ("digital flyer") on your profile along with the HTML code for showing the flyer. If you have a .jpg file of your album cover, you have a flyer created already. Have fans distribute it for you. Then fans can just copy and paste the code onto their Website to show your flyer, or into their Notes and HTML Box on Facebook!

Circulate a Digital Flyer Table 15.D
➢ Create the flyer using a graphic program such as Microsoft Paint and save in JPEG (.jpg) format ➢ Upload cover image to Facebook ➢ Use this HTML tag to show flyer on your profile: <a href="http://www.Facebook.com/BandURL" target="_blank"><img src="FACEBOOKURLOFCOVERIMAGE" width="319" height="413"></a> ➢ Display HTML under flyer; tell fans to copy and paste it onto their profile

51. List Groups Where Your Band Belongs

There are tons of cool groups out there. If your band belongs to some of them, why not list them on your profile? Be sure the group listing privacy setting is disabled.

52. Protect Band members From Posers

In developing the identity of your band it is just as important to guard against Facebook imposters. Facebook has a number of profiles where people pretend to be celebrities. If your band opts to have one profile with none of the individual members having their own profile, let the world know. Make it clear that band members do not have individual Facebook profiles of their own and further ask groupies to report any profile acting like it is one of your members.

53. Post Items for Sale on eBay

A lot of new bands offer CDs for sale on eBay.com to help out sales. If you are doing this, you can show these items on your profile so fans can click to buy them on eBay. Do not forget autographed memorabilia and band T-shirts, which are hot sellers.

Link to eBay Table 15.E
➤ Post item for sale on eBay → Visit profile on eBay where item is for sale ➤ Click in the browser URL window and copy the URL link ➤ Paste the link into any interest section of your profile and tell groupies to visit the link to buy your stuff

COOQY YOUR WAY TO SALES

Cooqy makes utilities for eBay buyers and sellers, including Website widgets that can be used for listing items. Visit cooqy.com today and launch your band product sales.

54. Post Items for Sale on Google Base

Google Base (www.base.google.com) has been cutting into eBay's business since its launch. One of the main reasons is because it does not charge for listing or selling items on the site. Google makes its money off click advertising. In addition, listing items on Google Base gets them automatically included in Google's search results.

Hyperlink to Google Base Table 15.F
➢ Post an item for sale on Google Base ➢ Visit page on Google Base where item is for sale ➢ Click in the browser URL window and copy the URL link ➢ Paste link into any interest section and tell groupies to click and buy

55. Upload New Songs Continuously

It's all about the music for most of your fans. To keep your band's profile sticky, upload new songs all the time using the Facebook Jukebox application. Upload a new song every month if possible. A few bands have even done one a week! So get writing and uploading to keep fans coming back for more.

56. Be a Fan of Bands in Your Genre

Does your band sound like 30 Seconds to Mars? How about P.O.D.? If you play music that sounds close to a famous band, get to be its fan. When you do, the fans of the popular band may click over to your profile and discover they like your tunes, too. Also remember to post comments as this will get you on the front page of the profile no matter how many friends the famous band has.

57. Pick a Prominent Friend Position

Facebook popularity is centered on how many friends you have; and not only the number of friends, which is very important, but also the quality of friends. What do we mean by the *quality* of friends? It is very simple. In the Facebook world the quality of friends is directly linked to their celebrity bling. Having movie stars, sports stars, and top-name bands as your groupies will launch your popularity. For better or worse, people are judged by the status level of their friends. Since friends appear on a person's profile in the order they were added, the first ones are placed at the top of a friends' list. This means visitors do not have to scroll to see them. They can click on the photo and go right to your profile where they can request to be added as your friend. Seek new friends (popular friends, better yet) that have just a few people shown on their profile to ensure top photo placement.

58. Join a Download Festival

A download music festival is a venue, similar to Lollapalooza, where various bands play. Download Festival is one of them.

It is a great way to let others download your music and discover you. Find out more at downloadfestival.com. Also be sure to search Facebook and use "download festival" as your keywords to learn what other bands have had success at the festival.

59. Hook Up with the Nemo Music Festival

As a music lover, 300 bands on 30 venues over 3 days sounds awesome. As a band, this is a great way to introduce yourself to potential new fans and to make friends with other bands.

There are also tons of industry moguls at these events that could launch your career if they like your sound. Get involved and get popular by playing at an event with big name acts. Also be sure to search Facebook and use the festival's name as your keywords to learn what other bands have had success at the festival.

60. Participate in a Video Competition

Musicnation.com hosts a video music competition each week for unsigned bands. Top bands pick a new winner that is posted and shown on the site each week and the overall winner gets a record deal with Epic.

Participate in a video music competition on Music Nation this week. You just might get tons free publicity for your band.

61. Watch for Undiscovered Band Contests

Movie profiles sometimes offer undiscovered band contests where groupies can vote for their favorites. Rockett Queen won the undiscovered band contest for the movie John Tucker Must Die.

Visit new movie profiles on the Web and enter your band in as many undiscovered band contests as possible. Who knows, you may win and be on your way to stardom.

62. Make Money Off Facebook Videos

There are a couple of great Websites where you can upload your band's videos and then the sites will share a percentage of the revenue when a person clicks on an Internet ad showing next to the video. If you have a popular video on Facebook, you are sitting on a digital moneymaking opportunity! People with popular videos have made thousands of dollars in click revenue off only one popular video. Listed below are the top video payment services and the amount of click revenue they will share with your band.

Video Sharing Website	Click Revenue Sharing Percentage
Revver.com	50%
eeFoof.com	50%
Panjea.com	50%
Blip.tv	50%

63. Get a Promoter/Publicity Manager

Having a professional outfit behind band promotions is key to success on Facebook. A great example is Cornerstone [Promotion], which can be found on the Web at cornerstonepromotion.com. It bills itself as "a lifestyle marketing company" and has helped many bands promote themselves on the Web, including Ice Cube. It is best if your publicity manager is already on Facebook and they know the site backwards and forwards. Your band needs someone who can tout your growing popularity to Facebook advertisers and work marketing deals for you. Search Facebook for "publicity manager" or "publicist".

64. Allow Snocap Downloads

Last, but certainly not least, there is a killer way to buzz your band through downloads right from your band's profile. In 2006 News Corp (the parent company of MySpace) became affiliated with Snocap Inc. (a music download startup company). Snocap allows songs to be downloaded with no DRM attached, meaning they are just plain old .mp3 files that can be used anywhere and on any portable device. Best of all, you can set the retail price per download.

To sign up for Snocap downloads go to snocap.com and create an account, then link your paypal.com account to Snocap for song payments.

BEST FOR BANDS THAT OWN COPYRIGHTS
Music downloads work best for bands that own the copyrights to their songs instead of a record label. That way bands can offer songs for $0.79 via Snocap without a record label complaining that the price is too low.

Search Facebook on the keyword "Snocap" to see if other bands have had success with paying downloads.

65. Record a Silent Movie Soundtrack

Don't know a filmmaker that will let you write a soundtrack? No problem. Just write your own for an old silent movie or video clip and post the video with your soundtrack. A soundtrack written for the old German silent film about Dracula called *Nosferatau* first popularized this on the Internet.

66. Enable the Amazon.com Honor System

What is the Amazon.com Honor System? It is a program where fans can give you money right on your Website by clicking on an Amazon link. Fans can give you as little as $1 USD at a time. This is a good way to fund your Website and to get money for all those free songs you are posting. Sign up at: http://zme.amazon.com/exec/varzea/fx-register/login.

Be sure to link to your Amazon.com Honor System page on your Facebook profile and let fans know that they can give money in support of your music.

67. Link Your Way to Success

Linking is the best way to get fans from your Facebook profile over to your Website. One click and they are there. While you are at it, ensure you hyperlink back from your Website to your Facebook profile. You can find a bunch of free linking icons that are provided by Facebook as Facebook Badges and with them you can provide a splashy graphic that lets the world click over to your Facebook profile. You have total control on what info you place in them. Got your own personal Website apart from Facebook? If so, this is a great place for your badge. Get started by clicking on Profile → Create a Profile Badge beneath your photo.

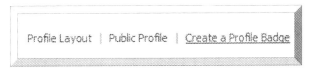

Steps to Get a Facebook Badge Table 15.G
➢ Login to Facebook ➢ Click on Profile ➢ Select create a profile badge under your photo

68. Publish Free Articles to Increase Profile Traffic

Post free articles about your films/short or filmmaking in general to generate free clicks over to your profile. That's right, there are a number of fine Websites that accept articles on filmmaking or most any general topic. Blogs and other sites may publish them on the Web for free and link back to your profile. Here is a list of some of the best ones: ContentDesk.com, Ezine Articles.com, GoArticles.com, and IdeaMarketers.com.

69. Win Battle of the Bands

Contests for bands are all about getting noticed. A Facebook app called Battle of the Bands pits bands against each other. Facebookers vote on their favorites.

Win it and you are on your way to getting noticed not just on Facebook, but by people in the industry outside of Facebook.

70. Have Fans Post Photos of Your Band
A good application for spreading your photo on Facebook is simply called Bands and with it people can insert pictures of bands on their profile.

Obviously all the big name bands are here and a few smaller ones. Contact the app's creators and make your band's photos available. Search Facebook for "Bands" to find the app. When you do, contact the creators and get free buzz generated for your band today!

71. Buzz with Babulous Bands
The Babulous Bands app lets you play your music, show videos for your band and list a bio all from the comfort of your Facebook profile.

This is a first rate way to show off the goods your band offers in a centralized place. Just search Facebook for "Babulous Bands" to add the application and get started.

72. Distribute with My Music
There is a hot app on Facebook that lets bands distribute their music in 6 currencies without paying commissions. The app is called My Music.

My Music

You can find it at: http://www.facebook.com/apps/application.php?id=2400548451&b. Follow the link to get started. One of the best features of the app lets you email limited-play, entire song previews to friends!

73. Sell Music with RawRip

Just like My Music, RawRip lets bands sell their music. With this application you sell directly from your Facebook profile to anyone who visits.

Get the app at: http://www.facebook.com/apps/application.php?id=2363363332&b, but first you must become a member of RawRip.com. Start ripping today and selling to Facebook fans!

What You'll Experience

Sponsor Films on Facebook

Do a Private Facebook Showing

Get Shorts on iTunes

Make Money Off Your Shorts

XVI   Buzz a Film

Want to become the next Scorsese, Spielberg, or Coppola? If you are an undiscovered filmmaker, it is crucial to get the attention you need to be discovered and Facebook is one of the places to do it. At your fingertips is a potential audience of over 30 million registered users! Do you want a crazy number of friends from all over the planet who worship your films? Have you ever wanted the power to sign with the studio of your choosing? Do you want to want to turn grassroots popularity into hard cash? If YES, sit back, strap yourself in and get ready to explode your film's popularity on Facebook with these tips and tricks. A number of them can also be used to buzz a band or a book on Facebook. We spell them out again as most filmmakers will not want to spend time reading how to buzz a band on Facebook.

1. Use the Correct Name

Having a name that is easy to remember on Facebook is important for your popularity and success. Sign up quickly to register your full name, which you use on your films, before an unofficial fan club or group takes it. If your name is already taken, get it as close to the name you promote as possible. For instance, if Pat Jones is the name you use as a filmmaker, register Patrick Jones if Pat Jones is already taken. You get the picture. If you are promoting your films to the public, now is not the time to be shy. You have the option to use only the first letter of your last name on Facebook for privacy reasons, and you will probably only use this option if you truncate your surname on films. Use your full first and last names if available.

2. Get Friends and More Friends

Facebook popularity, just like real life, is centered on how many friends you have. To get a ton of friends—we're talking hundreds—you cannot just sit back and wait for them to beat a path to your Facebook digital door. Remember this magic Facebook formula:

> **Friends = Fans => Even More Fans**

People become your friend on Facebook because they like your films or shorts. When they have made this fan-status leap of faith, they will work to get you even more fans. That is the beauty of Facebook when trying to quickly build your fan base. People love to show off they have discovered an awesome new filmmaker on Facebook. But this does not come overnight. Accept all the friend requests you receive and get this pile growing. As it does, so will your popularity.

3. Befriend the Stars

Stop hiding within the confines of your Facebook profile and get out there and try to *make* new friends. A great place to start is with movie stars. Most of the mega stars (Brad Pitt, Tom Cruise, Angelina Jolie, etc.) do not have Facebook profiles, yet a number of up and coming stars do have profiles to get their names out there and to establish a fan base, which is the lifeblood of a celebrity. They need you just as much or more than you need them.

If you get a famous friend, be sure to post a "Thanks for the Add" comment to get even more exposure at the popular profile.

AUTOMATIC CELEBRITY ADDS

Like many areas of their lives, celebrities have "their people" accept friend requests for them on Facebook. This "accept pretty much anyone who sends me a friend request" is your ticket to getting a celebrity as your friend.

Do not forget about non-movie/TV celebrities like sports stars (for some reason there is a lot of big-time wrestling stars on Facebook), authors, and comedians. Who knows, you may even be able to find a rising star to be in your next film.

4. Theme Your Profile

Your profile photo should reflect the theme of your latest film or short. Viewers want to believe in their filmmakers and the best shorts are often those experienced by the filmmaker in some fashion. If you have a partying photo on your profile, add a more serious one for your filmmaker profile to let everyone know you are a serious artist.

THIS INCLUDES ACTIVITIES & INTERESTS

The Activities and Interest areas of your profile are a great place to further build the theme of your latest work and the activities you've been participating in to research your next film or short. You have unlimited words to use for this purpose.

5. Hang with Popular Advertisements

Viral marketing is spreading on Facebook. Advertising characters are even showing up. As always, these are simply options. Most filmmakers will not want to be friends with big bad corporations or their advertising progeny. There are exceptions. Morgan Spurlock, filmmaker for the widely successful film *Super Size Me*, may want to be friends with Ronald McDonald to get people to see his film that pans the restaurant.

6. Add Profile URL to Email Messages

Your Facebook URL can easily be added to outgoing email messages in the form of a hyperlink that your non-Facebook friends can click on to be taken to your profile. If Facebook is your only Web presence, it's important to build up friends and fans on your profile. Below is an example with everything from the http to just before the first > being the Facebook profile URL.

```
Put a link to your Facebook profile on AIM:
<a href=http://www.facebook.com/p/Andy_B/527300036>Facebook me!</a>
```

Visit the URL chapter of *Facebook Fanatic* to learn how to add this link into the messages of the Web's most popular email engines.

7. Unlimited Words for Your Bio

Have film experience? Did you win first prize in a short competition? Have your films been shown in festivals? Did you graduate *cum laude* from film school? You have unlimited characters to use in the About section of your profile. Do not be shy. This is a great place to give your bio as a filmmaker.

> Another way to generate interest in your film or short is to provide a synopsis on your profile.

8. Let Your Feelings Be Known

Mom ever tell you to keep comments to yourself? Well, Facebook is not the place to follow Mom's instructions . . . if you want to become popular. Once you become friends with a celebrity or well-trafficked profile, send a comment over to keep your photo front and center. This includes other bands, films, movie characters, Notes, and groups. Be sure to show the cover art for your film or short and provide a link next to your photo.

LEAVE VIDEO COMMENTS

One of the hottest Facebook areas is the video section. If you find one that is a fit with your film, leave a comment and keep those clicks coming to your profile.

9. Keep in Touch on the Road

If you are touring the film circuit, broadcast the dates on your profile so fans new and old can see your flick. Create a quiz to show where you are playing next or write on your own Wall or post in Notes. Be creative.

With the Web portion of Facebook Mobile you can stay in touch with fans on the road. The graphics are sparse, but the meat of the matter is there for *all* sections of your profile. Mobile Web is where you can surf your Facebook profile at will. Always be connected! Did we mention that you can also stay in touch with the Events portion of Facebook? This is essential when on the road and you want to display where your films or shorts are playing next.

10. Add Photos and Notes on the Road

If you have some great pictures from last night's viewing, you can easily zap them to your Facebook profile by using Mobile Uploads. It is the coolest and quickest way to get info onto your Facebook profile when traveling. Want to send a blurb to Notes about the turn out you had at your gig last night while you are at it? No problem.

After your cellphone is enabled on Facebook, use these two email addresses: photos@facebooks.com and notes@facebook.com to upload photos and Notes, respectively.

11. SMS on the Road

Okay, so you can upload photos, update Events and send Notes on the road. Great. You can also SMS your fans using the handy commands below with Facebook SMS.

You can conduct your Facebook business by texting to FBOOK, which are the numbers 32665. Keep in mind that you can always text fans on Facebook even if they don't have a cellphone since your messages go right to their Facebook profile.

Action	Command	Example Text
Add a Friend	Add	Add Bob Marks
Fire a Friend	Fire	Fire Bob Marks
Get Cell Number	Cell	Cell Bob Marks
Message	Msg	Msg Bob Marks Are You Ready
Poke	Poke	Poke Bob Marks
Search Profile	N/A	Bob Marks
Wall Post	Wall	Wall Bob Marks Ace Your Exam
Write a Note	Note	Note Bob Marks Check Out www.TaleSale.com

12. Plan a Backyard Screening

Projector technology for PCs has gotten to such a level that you can now have outdoor film screenings. The old drive-in theatres are dead, but outdoor screenings are just getting started. All you have to do is get a projector and hook it to your laptop. Any large wall or tightly strung sheet will do. Notify your Facebook friends of this special screening. Even if they live faraway, it will help build buzz for your film.

> When you announce your screening, do not forget to put down on your profile how much it costs to attend the event.

13. Be a Note Hog

Notes are vital to making your profile "sticky" and for ensuring your films stay in the minds of viewers when tons of other films are trying to muscle you out. If you are doing screenings on the road, get a laptop with wireless Internet access so you can stay in touch with fans. Note every day or multiple times a day, letting them know when and where your films will be playing. Fans love to read about experiences on the road!

14. Post a Contest

A great way to get fans reading your Notes is to have contests periodically. How do you have one? Easy. State on your profile you will be having a Note contest in the next few weeks. Do not disclose the day. On the day you decide, post a trivia question about one of your films on your Note. The first one to answer the question correctly by leaving a comment gets an autographed T-shirt or DVD.

15. A Day in the Life

If you want to do a video that is between a music video and a movie, film a day in the life of a filmmaker and post it on Facebook. Watch The Beatles's "A Hard Day's Night" to see how they did it back in the day. Post the video on Facebook Diaries and watch your fans increase.

16. Post Short Videos

A hot short is one of the best ways to vault your popularity. If you have one, post it on your profile using Facebook Video. You should also post it on YouTube, AOL Video and Yahoo Video. Visit the video section of *Facebook Fanatic* to learn how to get a video from your camera or hard drive onto Facebook.

> At ffmpegx.com you can download free cellphone conversion software for the Mac.

Apple requires videos to be sized in a 640x480 format to play on video iPods. What is key to getting your shorts on mobile devices such as a cellphone or video iPod is to convert your video files into the correct format. Cellphones play video in 3GP format. For PCs Xilisoft has published its 3GP Converter at xilisoft.com for downloading. Keep the file size as small as possible to limit the download time on mobile devices. For video iPods there is a special iPod format. You can download MoviePod at nullriver.com in formats that work for the PC or Mac. The file can be of any size.

17. Upload Video Again

Let's say you already have cool short films uploaded to YouTube and don't want to upload it again to get it on your Facebook profile. This is a mistake. If you put a video directly on your profile by inserting the YouTube URL, it is easy to forget to also place the video within the video section of Facebook. By uploading a video directly to Facebook you can insert your own comments. You can also use the HTML Box application to show the YouTube video on your profile without uploading it again. Visit the video chapter of this book to learn more about this powerful application.

18. Post Movie Related Video

If you do not have a trailer or a short, post a video that is film related. For instance, if you toured MGM Studios, post the video.

POST A VIDEO FROM OTHER VIDEO SITES

Is there a sweet video on YouTube that shows great camera techniques? If you don't have a short, show one of these videos by inserting the YouTube URL into the HTML Box application after adding it to your Facebook profile.

19. Make a Video

What? Don't have a video? Some of the coolest videos are homemade and have a documentary feel. Many are shot in black and white. The jittery, unprofessional look is in style. You certainly do not need an expensive video camera for this. Use one lying around the apartment. Not sure how to post your short? Visit the video section of *Facebook Fanatic* to find out how.

20. Attach Video to Email Messages

It sounds complicated, but it is easy to attach videos or video interviews to email messages. Alternatively, you can always just copy the video URL and email or IM that link to your friends. Since it is a hyperlink, all they have to do is click on it to be taken to the Facebook profile where the video is showing.

21. Find a Popular Filmmaker

If you can befriend a popular filmmaker with a similar style, it is a great way to get new fans. How are you going to find a popular filmmaker on Facebook? Well, there are a number of ways to go about it. First, conduct a filmmaker search. This will pull up all types of filmmakers in every imaginable genre. A second, and more direct way to go about your search, is to look in filmmaker groups for your college, especially if it has a film school. If you cannot find any of merit, post a new topic and ask fellow alumnus if they know of any.

ATTEND FILM FESTIVALS OUT OF STATE

If you live in a small city that doesn't have film festivals, attend one when traveling. Contact in advance to see if you can get a showing. Tons are listed on Facebook.

22. Get a Free Soundtrack

Use great songs from unknown bands for your film soundtrack. These bands will jump over backwards to support your film and if the free advertising wasn't enough, the bands may not charge a royalty to get their music in a film. Hooking up with bands on Facebook is a great way to help each other out and to cross-pollinate your fan bases.

The All American Rejects scored the entire soundtrack for the movie "John Tucker Must Die".

23. Display URL for the Video

It is axiomatic that you want fans showing your trailers and shorts on their profiles. But you should also display the video URL or embedded code from YouTube on Facebook so fans can show it on their own Website if they have one.

24. Post Lyrics

Fans love to read the lyrics of songs on your film soundtrack. Post them on your profile to keep them coming back for more. Be sure to let the band know you are doing it and get their consent.

25. Conduct a Video Interview

The second best thing for fans other than watching your films and shorts is to watch a video interview by you. Gather around a pool table or sofa and record a video interview.

A LITTLE PLANNING IS GOOD

Get the questions laid out beforehand and think of what you are going to say so the video doesn't have to be cropped. Do not rehearse or you will sound canned.

Tip

26. Compile an Electronic Press Kit

Without leaving their wingback leather chairs, film producers and agents can check you out. That is the beauty of Facebook. Now you no longer need huge press kits filled with pictures, DVDs, and descriptions. All you need is a great profile with an electronic press kit and, of course, great films.

Key Items for a Digital Press Kit on Facebook Table 16.A
➢ Awards
➢ Biography
➢ Schooling
➢ Shorts accessible on profile
➢ Films accessible on profile
➢ Soundtracks
➢ Starter Images
➢ Screening dates, places and times

27. Get Signed With a Production Company

Getting signed with a production company is easier said than done. Receiving monetary backing for a film is difficult at best. There are simply no A-B-C steps to follow. Never fear. Your Facebook profile is your calling card to getting popular and recognized on Facebook. If it is unprofessional, no production companies will open their coffers to you. There is simply too much competition. Once you have a great profile with a digital press kit, search for producers on the Web and email them a hyperlink so they can click over to your profile. Visit the hyperlink section of *Facebook Fanatic* to learn how to automatically attach your link to messages on the major email engines.

CHECK OUT FILMMAKERS WITH A SIMILAR LOOK
If you find a filmmaker on Facebook with a similar look to their films and they have already signed with a producer, find out which one from their profile or DVD jacket. Then, approach a competitive company and market why your filmmaking is better. This is guerrilla film marketing at its finest.

28. Beat the digital Pavement

There is an old proverb that says they who want friends must make themselves friendly, or something like that. The same applies to Facebook. Stop hiding within the confines of your profile and get out there and try to *make* new friends to those who have film contacts on Facebook.

29. Make an iTunes Banner

Got a short on iTunes? Great! Create a graphic banner announcing it and place it on your Facebook profile. Be sure to put "Click to Buy on iTunes" or similar text across it. Use a URL link to point to the short. You do not want to have fans downloading other filmmaker's shorts (okay, we'll make an exception for Martin Scorsese) instead of yours as they browse iTunes.

30. Befriend Filmmaker Magazine

Are you an independent filmmaker? *Filmmaker Magazine* is all about promoting independent filmmakers. Each week it features a new filmmaker and provides info about their latest offerings.

31. Sell Stuff on QOOP

Viral marketing is spreading on Facebook. A great way to get in on the game is to sell photo items from QOOP. Never heard of it? Well, Facebook has teamed up with QOOP (QOOP.com), one of the Internet's leading photo printing services. With QOOP you can order photos, posters, etc. You name it and QOOP can usually print your photos on it. You can even order books of photos. Get creative and sell photos of yourself in many different ways on your Website, eBay or Facebook Marketplace.

32. Use Videos as a Stepping Stone

If you have a popular short getting lots of plays on Facebook, this is a great stepping stone over to your profile. If you create your short to tie into your film or as a trailer, it will greatly help sales of your film. Since all videos are hyperlinked in multiple areas to your profile (profile link, video cover or screen name), you will be on your way to increased traffic and sales!

STARTER IMAGE IS KEY

Tweak the starter image for your video and see if this changes your play-per-view ratio. Sometimes a very small change will get more visitors watching your video.

Tip

33. Focus on Favorite Movies

The Favorite Movies area of your interest section is important for filmmakers. Here is where you show what films inspire you. Fans like to see what makes their filmmaker's tick. So pay adequate attention to this area. Stick your own film in there, of course, if you have one.

34. Show Off Fans

Just like profile views and video plays, the number of fans you have as a filmmaker is very important. Tons of fans along with a great video can get you linked to a production company.

35. Do a Private Showing on Facebook

Want to reward fans with a private screening or a new short? This is easy. Post a Note announcing the video and when your fans will be able to view it. All you have to do is upload it to Facebook at the designated time and date.

36. Publish Free Articles to Increase Profile Traffic

Post free articles about your films/short or filmmaking in general to generate free clicks over to your profile. That's right, there are a number of fine Websites that accept articles on filmmaking or most any general topic. Blogs and other sites may publish them on the Web for free and link back to your profile. Here is a list of some of the best ones: ContentDesk.com, Ezine Articles.com, GoArticles.com, and IdeaMarketers.com.

37. Have a Facebook Band Do Your Soundtrack

There are tons of new bands on Facebook trying to break into the business just as you are trying to do in the film area. Contact a few before your film is in production and see if they will create a soundtrack for it. Most small bands will do it for little or no money to get exposure. This is a great way to cross-pollinate fan bases.

38. Start a Group About Your Film

Facebook groups are a fantastic way to get film noticed. If you attended a school (especially a film school) that has a group, this is a good place to get known. Also, if you were in a fraternity/sorority, this is a good category to get your name out. You should also ask fans to start a group, if they desire. If your films have a fan club group, post in it regularly! The fans will love this. You should also post in groups that discuss the theme of one of your films like noir films, etc.

39. Post Link to Your Group on Profile

You can always post a quick link to the group you started (or fans started) on Facebook. Keep in mind that you can only join groups for schools or colleges that you attended, but there may be other groups about your films in other schools and colleges. Ask fans in your Notes to send you links to these groups so you can include them on your profile.

40. Become a Member of a Group

Even if you do have a group dedicated to your films, it is always good to post in a film-related group within your school or college on Facebook. There are also unofficial profiles that have turned themselves into video and short film groups on Facebook. Be sure to search for these also.

41. Create "Share on Facebook" HTML

Facebook provides you a basic Share on Facebook HTML link to put on your Website. This makes it easy for visitors to click it and share the content on Facebook with their friends. Fine. But if you really want to make HTML links come alive, there are special HTML meta tags that you must insert to preview the content. See the Posted Items chapter of *Facebook Fanatic* for linking options. The minor problem with sharing content using these links is that they only provide a link and little else. There are no meta tags that tell Facebook what type of content it is (audio, video, image, text, etc.). Add the following basic tags to ensure the title of your film and description are imported into Facebook. This also includes the initial image of your film or short.

Meta Tags

<meta name="title" content="'AdSense Unleashed' book published by BottleTree" />
<meta name="description" content="Learn the tips you need to make money by showing free Google ads on your

> The title and summary tags are the minimum requirements for any preview, so make sure to include these two.

Website." />
<link rel="image_src" href="http://www.bottletreebooks.com/AdsenseUnleashed.jpg" />

Basic Content Tags

An example short story could have the following:
<meta name="title" content="The Legend of Sleepy Hollow" />
<meta name="description" content="Icabod Crain and the Headless Horseman. Need we say more?" />
<link rel="image_src" href="URLofCOVERIMAGE.jpg" />
As shown, title contains the preview title, description contains the preview summary and image_src contains the preview image.

Type of Content Tag

You may specify the type of content being shared by using the following tag:
<meta name="medium" content="medium_type" />
Valid values for *medium_type* are "audio", "image", "video", "news", "Note" and "mult".

* To make videos embeddable on Facebook, please send a request to developers-help@facebook.com. This request should include the domain names of the values you will use for the video source URL (in the video_src link tag above). You must do this to ensure your videos play correctly.

42. Circulate a Flyer

We've all seen how big name politicians plaster TV commercials and national newspapers with the latest advertising. Now, even if you are a small filmmaker, you can do the same thing, but digitally. All it takes is for you to post an image ("digital flyer") on your profile along with the HTML code for showing the flyer. Then fans can just copy and paste the code onto their Websites to show it!

Circulate a Digital Flyer Table 16.B
➤ Create flyer using a graphics program like Microsoft Paint and save in PNG format ➤ Upload flyer to an image hosting site like Photo Bucket (<u>photobucket.com</u>) ➤ Use this HTML tag to show flyer on your profile: <a href="http://www.Facebook.com/URL" target="_blank"><img src="http://i16.photobucket.com/albums/NAMEofFILMMAKER/NAMEofFLYER.png" width="319" height="413"></a> ➤ Display HTML under the flyer and tell fans to paste it onto their Website

43. List Groups

There are tons of cool groups out there. If you belong to some of them that are film related, why not list them on your profile? Ensure these groups relate to your style or genre and will not turn off fans.

44. Submit to a Short Festival

There are film festivals out there dedicated to shorts. They come in all variations with anime being very popular.

SUBMIT TO FREE FESTIVALS

If you are struggling to make money off your shorts, it is hard to keep paying entrance fees. Many great festivals do not charge a fee for new shorts or films. Focus on these first.

45. Get Noticed at a Film Festival

Facebook is all about videos and their promotion. By submitting your work, this is one of the best ways to get recognized on Facebook and become popular. Film festivals are a great way to do it outside of Facebook. It is common for industry professionals to attend the top film festivals, so begin submitting today!

MOST FILM FESTIVALS DISPLAY SHORTS

If you are a newbie filmmaker and only have shorts, do not overlook film festivals. Many of them also have a shorts section like the Slamdance festival.

46. Protect Yourself From Posers

In developing your filmmaker identity, it is just as important to guard against Facebook imposters. Facebook has profiles with people pretending to be celebrities or filmmakers. State at the top of your profile that this is your "official" profile and that no others exist on Facebook.

47. Post Items for Sale on eBay

As a filmmaker you can offer DVDs for sale on eBay.com to help out sales. If you are doing this, show these items on your profile too so fans can click to buy your DVDs. Do not forget autographed memorabilia and T-shirts, which are always hot sellers.

Hyperlink to eBay Table 16.C
➢ Post item for sale on eBay ➢ Visit page on eBay where item is for sale ➢ Copy and paste the URL link into your profile

48. Post Items for Sale on Google Base

Google Base (www.base.google.com) has been cutting into eBay's business because it does not charge for listing or selling items on the site. Google makes its money off click advertising. In addition, listing items on Google Base gets them automatically included in Google's search results.

Hyperlink to Google Base Table 16.D
➢ Post item for sale on Google Base
➢ Visit page on Google Base where item is for sale
➢ Click in the browser URL window and copy the URL link
➢ Paste the Google Base URL into your profile

49. Free Your Films

When you are struggling to make it as a filmmaker, it seems counterintuitive to give away your first short. But this is one of the best ways to get new fans. Let Facebook users watch your shorts for free and share them with others. When you do, watch your popularity increase.

50. Upload New Shorts Continuously

It's all about the videos for most of your fans. To keep your profile sticky, upload new shorts all the time. Upload a new short every month if possible. So get shooting and uploading to keep fans coming back for more.

51. Make a Few Polls

Polls are a good way to focus the attention of Facebookers on a particular topic for your film or short. The best polls have one question and contain between 2 and 5 possible answers. Notes is a great place to conduct a poll or by leaving the poll question in a comment on The Wall.

FILMMAKER POLL

Do a poll about yourself. This is a good way to generate fan base interaction and to gage what fans would like to see from you in the future.

Here are some other poll ideas. Most are general in nature, but will make your profile sticky.

Great Poll Ideas
Table 16.E
➢ Trivia about your favorite, movie, TV show, etc.
➢ Who is the best actor?
➢ What is your dream film about?
➢ What do you fear the most?
➢ Questions about the best city or place to go on vacation
➢ Which amusement park has the best rollercoasters?
➢ Best pickup line
➢ Worst pickup line
➢ Who will win a sporting event or election?
➢ Best chick flick
➢ Best book of the last 100 years (Hint: *Catcher in the Rye*)
➢ Prime location to get a tattoo
➢ Coolest tattoo

52. Use Cover for Profile Image

If your film or short is not widely available, scan in a cover of your DVD and get it on your profile. Instead of showing your face as the default profile picture, show your DVD cover. This is a great way to make your photo stand apart from the thousands of faces on Facebook as people browse through them.

53. Join the IMDb

The Internet Movie Database is a free Website with unbelievable content on all information relating to films and filmmakers. It also offers content.

Visit the IMDb today and ensure your information is correct. Add new data, including content and links to your Facebook profile. Find out more at imdb.com. Last, link to your IMDb listing from your Facebook profile by providing the unique URL in your profile.

54. Link to Amazon Unbox

In 2006 Amazon.com launched Unbox and began offering film and short content for download on its Website: unbox.com.

This is huge for you as a filmmaker since Amazon is open to discovering great new films and shorts. Once you get content on Unbox, be sure to link to it from your Facebook profile. Happy uploading!

HOW TO CONTACT AMAZON UNBOX

To get your film or short uploaded onto Unbox, you must first contact Amazon by email and give basic information regarding format, length, genre, type, etc at: dv-original-content-inquiry@amazon.com.

55. Watch for Undiscovered Filmmaker Contests

Search for undiscovered filmmaker contests on Facebook where fans can vote for their favorites. This is especially true for films consisting of a group of compiled shorts. Visit movie page profiles that are new to Facebook and enter yourself in as many undiscovered filmmaker contests as possible. Who knows, you may win and be on your way to stardom. Check out sponsored videos, too.

56. Make Money Off Facebook Videos

There are a couple of great Websites that will let you upload videos. The sites share a percentage of the revenue when a person clicks on an Internet ad next to the video. If you have a popular short on Facebook, you are sitting on a digital moneymaking opportunity! People with popular videos have made thousands of dollars in click revenue off only one popular video. Listed below are the top video payment services and the amount of click revenue they share with you.

Video Sharing Website	Click Revenue Sharing Percentage
Revver.com	50%
eeFoof.com	50%
Panjea.com	50%
Blip.tv	50%

57. Enable the Amazon.com Honor System

What is the Amazon.com Honor System? It is a program where fans can give you money right on your Website by clicking on the link. Fans can give you as little as $1

USD at a time. This is a good way to fund your Website and to get money for all those free shorts you are posting. To sign up for the system follow this link: http://zme.amazon.com/exec/varzea/fx-register/login.

58. Get Short Mobile

Linking is the best way to get fans from your Facebook profile over to your Website. One click and they are there. While you are at it, ensure you hyperlink back from your Website to your Facebook profile. You can find a bunch of free linking icons that are provided by Facebook as Facebook Badges and with them you can provide a splashy graphic that lets the world click over to your Facebook profile. You have total control on what info you place in them. Got your own personal Website apart from Facebook? If so, this is a great place for your badge.

Steps to Get a Facebook Badge Table 16.F
➢ Login to Facebook ➢ Click on Profile ➢ Select create a profile badge under your photo

59. Post List of Questions

Another good way to buzz a film on Facebook is to include a list of questions for groups and classes so that they can discuss your film. Create a new Note entry on your profile and list out a bunch of questions for discussion. Then you can list the answers to these questions at a later time and see if they agree with those discussed by the group or class.

60. List a Great Quiz

Publish a quiz about yourself or your films. Let's say you don't want to publish a quiz about yourself or your films, you just want to keep things interesting on your profile. The options for alternate quizzes are only limited by your imagination. Name your quiz whatever you would like and start creating it. Here are some rad ideas to get you started.

Great Quiz Ideas Table 16.G
➤ Trivia about your favorite band, movie, TV show, sports team, book, etc. ➤ Questions about your school are cool. ➤ Any quiz about the theme of your profile (fast cars, basketball, Goth, etc.). ➤ Random quiz with questions about all kinds of different topics to see how smart your visitors are. ➤ Good in math? Create a math quiz. ➤ Make an anagram quiz by arranging letters of, for example, the name of popular authors (e.g., HONKS A JET = John Keats; A SHEEP'S RAKE = Shakespeare). Four potential answers are given and the right one must be guessed. ➤ Ask trivia about your friends and the results will be reported to you via email. This is a great way to find out intimate details about your friends!

SEARCH THE NET

A search of the Internet for "Quiz Ideas" or "Quiz Questions" will yield some great quiz Websites that will help you build cool quizzes. Why not start today?

What You'll Experience

Promote Events on Facebook

Increase Online Donations

Stave Off Imposters

Create an Electronic Press Kit

XVII   Zoom a Campaign

Are you the next Lincoln or Lyndon Johnson? Do want to be your next class president or head of your sorority? Political campaigns have never seemingly been so important as they are today and ever increasing pressure is being applied at local, state and federal levels to succeed. That's why it is crucial to get the attention you need and Facebook is one of the best places to do it. At your fingertips is a potential audience of over 30 million registered users! Search Facebook and you will find profiles for democrats, republicans, socialists and even communists. In this chapter you will learn how to zoom your political campaign on Facebook with over 40 tips and tricks to get your political campaign noticed, get voters, attract volunteers and raise donations.

1. Use the Most Recognized Name

Having a name that is easy to remember on Facebook is important for your popularity and success. Sign up quickly to register your full name, which you use on your campaign trail, before an opponent takes it. If your name is already taken, get it as close to the name you promote as possible. For instance, if Pat Jones is the name you use as a politician, register Patrick Jones if Pat Jones is already taken. You get the picture. If you are promoting your stories in the public, now is not the time to be shy. You have the option to use only the first letter of your last name on Facebook for privacy reasons, but this does not apply to politicians in most cases. Use your full first and last names.

2. Get Friends and More Friends

Facebook popularity, just like real life, is centered on how many voter friends you have. To get a ton of friends—we're talking hundreds, if not thousands—you cannot just sit back and wait for them to come and beat a path to your Facebook digital door. Remember this simple Facebook formula:

> **Friends = Voters => Even More Voters**

People become your friend on Facebook because they agree with your political stance on the issues. When they become your friend it has been shown that they will work to get you even more voters. This is volunteerism at its best and that is the beauty of Facebook when trying to quickly build your base of voters. But this does not come overnight. Accept all friend requests and get this pile growing.

3. Theme Your Profile Photo

Nobody wants to see a stodgy politician's photo on Facebook. This is not your grandfather's Website. Your profile photo should reflect the theme of your campaign and bring you down to earth. Voters want to believe that you are a real person.

THIS INCLUDES ACTIVITIES & INTERESTS

The Activities and Interest areas of your profile are a great place to further build the theme of your book and the activities you've been participating in to bolster the theme of your campaign. You have unlimited words to use for this purpose.

4. Create Great Polls

Politicians are familiar with the phrase "going to the polls", but this is the Facebook world and there is another type of poll that will keep your name in front of voters on election day. The EasyVote application is a great way to create free polls on your profile.

Easy ✓ote

free polls

Polls are a good way to focus the attention of voters on a particular topic for your campaign. The best polls have one question and contain between 2 and 5 possible answers. Notes is also a great place to conduct a poll. You can also leave a poll in a comment on The Wall for others to comment on later.

POLITICIAN POLL

Do a poll about yourself. This is a good way to generate voter interaction and to gage what readers would like to see from you in the future.

Here are some other poll ideas. Most are general in nature, but will make your profile sticky.

Great Poll Ideas Table 17.A
➢ Trivia about your favorite band, movie, TV show, sports team, book, etc.
➢ Who is the best athlete?
➢ What is your dream car?
➢ What do you fear the most?
➢ Questions about the best city or place to go on vacation
➢ Which amusement park has the best rollercoasters?
➢ Best pickup line
➢ Worst pickup line
➢ Who will win a sporting event or election?
➢ Best chick flick
➢ Best book of the last 100 years (Hint: *Catcher in the Rye*)
➢ Prime location to get a tattoo
➢ Coolest tattoo

5. Create Votes on Any Issue

Most voters are familiar with the major issues, but polls have shown that many are unaware about their candidate's stance on so-called minor or sub-issues. Now there is a way to create a vote on your profile about any issue using the Vote application.

With this powerful app you can create a vote on any topic. Use it to feel out voters early in your campaign to see how they would like you to take a stance on important sub-issues. Conduct a Facebook search on "Vote Application" to find it.

6. Let Feelings Be Known

Once you become friends with a celebrity or well-trafficked profile, send a comment over to keep your photo in the front and center. This includes authors, filmmakers, Notes, and groups.

LEAVE VIDEO COMMENTS

One of the hottest Facebook areas is the video section. If you find one that is a fit with your political views, leave a comment and keep those clicks coming.

You have to get out there and cast your photo/comments net in as many popular places as possible to catch the most friends. This is "pressing the flesh" digital style. If you are casting your net in shallow waters by making a few friend requests a day, you're not going to catch big fish. A great way to catch that digital mackerel is to become friends with popular profiles.

7. List Your Bio

You have unlimited characters to use in the About Me section of your profile. Do not be shy. This is a great place to give a full biography relating to your political career.

NAME DROPPING IS OKAY
If during your political career you have crossed paths with a famous politician or person favored by your political party, be sure to tell the world in your biography.

8. Post a List of Trivia
To make your profile more engaging to younger folks on Facebook, post a list of trivia about yourself on your profile. This is also a great way to get voters to remember key facts about you.

9. Let Voters Into Your Life
Making public your personal life is a good way to breach the politician barrier and make you come across as the real person that you are. Got a weakness for New Jersey cheese bagels or Memphis BBQ? Tell everyone on your profile. Show your human side and watch voters increase as friends. Voters want to be able to relate to whom they vote for on a personal level.

10. Email Voters
Speaking at a banquet in Chicago or London? If so, send a Facebook message to voters reminding them if they have not visited your profile in a few weeks. Also have them check out the events section of your profile where you should list your speaking engagements.

11. Show Pet Photos
Photos of you shaking hands with voters or standing in front of a flag are fine, but to show your personal side, post a photo of your pet. Voters love to see Fido or Fluffy doing their thing on Facebook.

12. Post a Video Reading
The coolest thing in politics has nothing to do with paper or ink. It is actually a way you can do selected readings, speeches or even spoofs. Videos are all the rage. Do one and post it on Facebook or YouTube. Some of the coolest videos are homemade with a documentary feel. Many are shot in black and white. You certainly do not need an expensive video camera for this. Visit the video section of *Facebook Fanatic* to learn how to get a video from your camera or hard drive onto Facebook. You should also target your video for mobile devices. What is key to getting your videos on mobile devices such as a cellphone or video iPod is to convert your video files into the correct

format. Cellphones play video in 3GP format. For PCs Xilisoft has published its 3GP Converter at xilisoft.com for downloading. Keep the file size as small as possible to limit the download time on mobile devices.

For video iPods there is a special iPod format. You can download MoviePod at nullriver.com in formats that work for the PC or Mac. The file can be of any size. Apple requires all films and shorts to be sized in a 640x480 format to play on video iPods.

> At ffmpegx.com you can download free cellphone conversion software for the Mac.

13. Post a Contest
A great way to get fans reading your Notes is to have periodic contests. How do you have one? Easy. State on your profile you will be having a Note contest in the next few weeks. On the day you decide, post a trivia question about yourself or your pet, etc on your Note. The first one to answer correctly by leaving a comment gets an autographed photo.

14. Get a Publicity Manager
Having a professional outfit behind you for Facebook promotion is key to your political success. It is best if your publicity manager is already on Facebook and they know the site backwards and forwards. You need someone who can tout your growing popularity to Facebook advertisers and work marketing deals for you. Search Facebook for "publicity manager" or "publicist". This could be a great opportunity for you to make money for your campaign while speaking on the road.

15. Note Trivia
In some circles political Notes are viewed as boring. To attract attention to Notes, be sure to post trivia about your personal life. Can you do a stupid trick? Tell the world. Do not short change voters on the lighter aspects of your life. Notes on Facebook are also a good place to conduct an interview. The entire interview will be shown on your profile for all to read.

16. Place Video on Profile
By placing your video on your Facebook profile, fans can watch it at any time. Visit the video section of *Facebook Fanatic* to learn how to get a video onto your profile using Facebook Video or the HTML Box application. It's easy.

17. Post a Political Video
If at the moment you do not have a video of yourself, post a video that is politically related from a key figure in your party.

POST A VIDEO FROM YOUTUBE
Is there a sweet political video on YouTube? If you don't have a video of yourself, show one of these videos by placing it in your HTML Box.

18. Make a Video

Some of the coolest videos are homemade and have a documentary feel. Many are shot of the politician while speaking to a group of supporters. You certainly do not need an expensive video camera for this. Use one lying around the office. Not sure how to post your video? Visit the video section of *Facebook Fanatic* to find out how. What is key to getting your videos on mobile devices such as a cellphone or video iPod is to convert your video files into the correct format. Cellphones play video in 3GP format. For PCs Xilisoft has published its 3GP Converter at xilisoft.com for downloading. Keep the file size as small as possible to limit the download time on mobile devices.

> At ffmpegx.com you can download free cellphone conversion software for the Mac.

For video iPods there is a special iPod format. You can download MoviePod at nullriver.com in formats that work for the PC or Mac. The file can be of any size. Apple requires all films and shorts to be sized in a 640x480 format to play on video iPods.

19. Attach Video to Email Messages

It sounds complicated, but it is easy to attach video to email messages. Alternatively, you can always just copy the video URL and email or IM that link to voters. Since it is a hyperlink, all they have to do is click on the link to be taken to the Facebook profile where the video is showing. If your video is posted only on YouTube, just copy that URL and do the same.

20. Publish Free Articles to Increase Profile Traffic

Post free articles about your campaign to generate clicks over to your profile. That's right, there are a number of fine Websites that accept articles on politics or most any general topic. Blogs and other sites may publish them on the Web for free and link back to your profile. Here is a list of some of the best ones: ContentDesk.com, Ezine Articles.com, GoArticles.com, and IdeaMarketers.com.

21. Circulate a Flyer

We've all seen how big name politicians plaster TV commercials and national newspapers with the latest advertising. Now, even if you are a small politician, you can do the same thing, but digitally. All it takes is for you to post an image ("digital flyer") on your profile along with the HTML code for showing the flyer. Then voters can just copy and paste the code onto their Websites to show it!

Circulate a Digital Flyer Table 17.B
➤ Create the flyer using a graphic program such as Microsoft Paint and save in JPEG (.jpg) format ➤ Upload flyer to an image hosting site like Photo Bucket (photobucket.com) ➤ Use this HTML tag to show flyer on your profile: <a href="http://www.Facebook.com/URL" target="_blank"><img src="http://i16.photobucket.com/albums/NAMEofPOLITICIAN/NAMEofFLYER.jpg" width="319" height="413"></a> ➤ Display HTML under the flyer and tell voters to paste it onto their Website

22. Conduct a Video Interview

Sit behind (or on) your favorite desk or in front of a bookcase and record a video interview. The person behind the camera can ask the questions.

A LITTLE PLANNING IS GOOD

Get questions laid out beforehand and think of what you are going to say so the video does not have to be cropped. Being smooth has its advantages, especially in politics.

Tip

23. Get Donations

The Vote on the Book application simulates the 2008 Presidential Election in the United States and allows for money to be donated to the candidates.

Each Facebooker who votes donates money to their candidate. Preview the election before it happens! Search Facebook for "Vote on the Book" application.

24. Add Facebook URL to Email Messages

Your Facebook URL can easily be added to outgoing email messages in the form of a hyperlink that your non-Facebook friends can click on to be taken to your profile. If Facebook is your only Web presence, it's important to build up friends and fans on your profile. Below is an example with everything from the http to just before the first > being the Facebook profile URL.

> Put a link to your Facebook profile on AIM:
> <a href=http://www.facebook.com/p/Andy_B/527300036>Facebook me!</a>

Visit the URL chapter of *Facebook Fanatic* to learn how to add this link into the messages of the Web's most popular email engines.

25. Compile an Electronic Press Kit

The beauty of Facebook is that you no longer have to physically print a press kit filled with pictures and a lengthy bio when you can have a much better (and less expensive) one on your profile. It is up to you to find out how to distribute your political buttons!

Key Items for a Digital Press Kit on Facebook Table 17.C
➢ Biography
➢ Photos
➢ Education
➢ Experience
➢ Videos
➢ Awards
➢ Publications or writing samples
➢ Speaking engagements

26. Do Not Forget Videos of the Competition

You may think it is a huge mistake to show a video of the competitor on your Facebook profile. This is not the case if there is an embarrassing video of him or her on the Web. If you have decided to include negative ads in your campaign, posting a video of your competitor making a fool of themselves works great on a profile.

27. Be a Note Hog

Notes are vital to making your profile "sticky" and for ensuring your writing stays in the minds of voters when lots of other politicians are trying to muscle you out. If you are doing events on the road, get a laptop with wireless Internet access so you can stay in touch with voters. Post a Note every day or multiple times a day, letting them know when and where you will be doing the next event. Notes should become second nature. Voters love to read your experiences on the road! Be sure to create a URL hyperlink at the end of your Note.

CONDUCT AN INTERVIEW ON YOUR NOTE

On your profile conduct an interview in question-and-answer fashion. Do it in Notes and watch your support base grow. This is popular for authors to do, too.

28. Sell Photos on QOOP

Viral marketing is spreading on Facebook. A great way to get in on the game is to sell photo items from QOOP. Never heard of it? Well, Facebook has teamed up with QOOP (QOOP.com), one of the Web's leading photo printing services. With QOOP you can order photos, posters, etc. You name it and QOOP can usually print your photos on it. You can even order books of photos. This is a great way to publish that photo book you've wanted to put out there. Get creative and sell photos of yourself in many different ways on your Website, eBay or Facebook Marketplace.

29. Circulate a Digital Poster

We've all seen how big name politicians plaster magazines and national newspapers with their latest ads. Now, even if you are a new politician, you can do the same thing, but digitally, and reach the entire world. All it takes is for you to post an image ("digital flyer") on your profile along with the HTML code for showing the flyer. If you have a .jpg file of your campaign photo, you have a flyer created already. Have supporters distribute it for you. Then voters can just copy and paste the code onto their Website to show your flyer. They can also copy and paste it into their Notes and HTML Box on Facebook!

Circulate a Digital Flyer
Table 17.D
➤ Create the flyer using a graphic program such as Microsoft Paint and save in JPEG (.jpg) format
➤ Upload cover image to Facebook
➤ Use this HTML tag to show flyer on your profile: <a href="http://www.Facebook.com/PoliticianURL" target="_blank"><img src="FACEBOOKURLOFIMAGE" width="319" height="413"></a>
➤ Display HTML under flyer and tell voters to paste it onto their Website

30. Hyperlink to Success

URL linking is the best way to get voters from your Facebook profile over to your Website. A copy and paste into their browser window and they are there. While you are at it, ensure you hyperlink back from your Website to your Facebook profile.

31. Start a Group About Politics

Facebook groups are a fantastic way to get noticed. If you attended a school that has a group, this is a good place to get known. Also, if you were in a fraternity/sorority, this is a good area to get your name out. There are many places where you can start a group about politics. You should also ask voters to start their own group if they desire. If a voter group about you is started, post in it regularly! Voters will love it. You should also post in groups that discuss the theme of your political ideals.

32. Protect Persona From Posers

In developing your identity as a politician, it is just as important to guard against Facebook imposters. People like to pretend to be politicians on Facebook.

OFFICIAL PAGE

So there is no confusion with pundit profiles, state in the about section or even your screen name that this is your "official" Facebook profile. Lock down your persona on Facebook.

33. Post Items for Sale on eBay

Politicians offer signed photos and T-shirts for sale on eBay.com to help out funding. If you are doing this, you can provide a link to these items on your profile too, so voters can click to buy. It is estimated that a message on a T-shirt is viewed over 3000 times before the T-shirt is tossed aside.

Link to eBay
Table 17.E
➢ Post item for sale on eBay
➢ Visit page on eBay where item is for sale
➢ Click in the browser URL window and copy the URL link
➢ Paste the URL into your Facebook profile

34. Post Items for Sale on Google Base

Google Base (www.base.google.com) has been cutting into eBay's business. One of the main reasons is because it does not charge for listing or selling items. Google makes its money off click advertising. In addition, listing items on Google Base gets them automatically included in Google's search results.

Link to Google Base
Table 17.F
➢ Post item for sale on Google Base
➢ Visit page on Google Base where item is for sale
➢ Click in the browser URL window and copy the URL link
➢ Paste the link into your Facebook profile

35. Enable the Amazon.com Honor System

What is the Amazon.com Honor System? It is a program where supporters can give you money right on your Website by clicking on the link. Supporters can give you as little as $1 USD at a time. This is a good way to fund your Website and add campaign money. To sign up follow this link: http://zme.amazon.com/exec/varzea/fx-register/login.

Be sure to link to your Amazon.com Honor System page on Facebook and let profile visitors know that they can give money in support of your political campaign.

36. Make Money Off Facebook Videos

There are a couple of great Websites that will share a percentage of the revenue when a person clicks on an ad showing next to your video. If you have a popular video on Facebook, you are sitting on a digital moneymaking opportunity for your political campaign! People with popular videos have made thousands of dollars in click revenue.

Listed below are the top video payment services and the amount of click revenue they will share with you.

Video Sharing Website	Click Revenue Sharing Percentage
Revver.com	50%
eeFoof.com	50%
Panjea.com	50%
Blip.tv	50%

MAKE MONEY OFF OPPONENT SNAFUS

If you have video of your bitter political rival embarrassing himself or herself, you can always make money by showing it on the sites above. A double whammy!

37. Rock the Vote

Rock the Vote is not a Facebook application but actually a group where you must get involved as a politician in a worthy effort to get your name out there.

To find the group just search "Rock the Vote" on Facebook and it will pop right up. Join, get involved and post regularly.

38. Sell Text and Audio Speeches on TaleSale

TaleSale.com is a great Website that lets anyone sell speeches in PDF format or audio speeches in MP3 format. Launching in late 2007, TaleSale creates a community of politicians and voters.

Get a profile on TaleSale.com and start selling the text and audio of your speeches. Not only will you make money for your campaign, but you will enable supporters to listen to your speeches while they work out and do yard chores.

39. Create "Share on Facebook" HTML

Facebook provides you a basic Share on Facebook HTML link to put on your Website. This makes it easy for voters to click it and share the content on Facebook with their friends. Fine. But if you really want to make HTML links come alive, there are special HTML meta tags that you must insert to preview the content. See the Posted Items chapter of *Facebook Fanatic* for linking options. The minor problem with sharing content using these links is that they only provide a link and little else. There are no meta tags that tell Facebook what type of content it is (audio, video, image, text, etc.). Add the following basic tags to ensure the title of your speech and a short description are imported into Facebook. This also includes the initial image of your content, if it is an image or video, which is displayed on Facebook. Here's a book example.

Meta Tags
<meta name="title" content="'AdSense Unleashed' book published by BottleTree" />
<meta name="description" content="Learn the tips you need to make money by showing free Google ads on your Website." />
<link rel="image_src" href="http://www.bottletreebooks.com/AdsenseUnleashed.jpg" />

Basic Content Tags
An example short story could have the following:
<meta name="title" content="The Legend of Sleepy Hollow" />
<meta name="description" content="Icabod Crain and the Headless Horseman. Need we say more?" />
<link rel="image_src" href="URLofCOVERIMAGE.jpg" />

> The title and summary tags are the minimum requirements for any preview, so make sure to include these two.

As shown, title contains the preview title, description contains the preview summary and image_src contains the preview image.

Type of Content Tag
You may specify the type of content being shared by using the following tag:
<meta name="medium" content="medium_type" />
Valid values for *medium_type* are "audio", "image", "video", "news", "Note" and "mult".

* To make videos embeddable on Facebook, please send a request to developers-help@facebook.com. This request should include the domain names of the values you will use for the video source URL (in the video_src link tag above). You must do this to ensure your videos play correctly.

40. Have a Facebook Filmmaker Use Your Story

There are tons of new and independent filmmakers on Facebook trying to break into the business just as you are trying to do in politics. Contact a few and see if they would like a royalty free license to use your story in an upcoming short film. It's not as hard as it sounds to find a filmmaker on Facebook, especially if they are a supporter of your political ideals.

41. List a Great Quiz

Publish a quiz about yourself or your campaign. To keep yourself viewed as a real person, you may just want to keep things interesting on your profile. The options for alternate quizzes are only limited by your imagination. Name your quiz whatever you would like and start creating it. Here are some rad ideas to get you started.

Great Quiz Ideas Table 17.G
➢ Trivia about your favorite band, movie, TV show, sports team, book, etc.
➢ Questions about your school are cool.
➢ Any quiz about the theme of your profile (fast cars, basketball, Goth, etc.).
➢ Random quiz with questions about all kinds of different topics to see how smart your visitors are.
➢ Good in math? Create a math quiz.
➢ Make an anagram quiz by arranging letters of, for example, the name of popular authors (e.g., HONKS A JET = John Keats; A SHEEP'S RAKE = Shakespeare). Four potential answers are given and the right one must be guessed.
➢ Ask trivia about your friends and the results will be reported to you via email. This is a great way to find out intimate details about your friends!

SEARCH THE NET

A search of the Internet for "Quiz Ideas" or "Quiz Questions" will yield some great quiz Websites that will help you build cool quizzes. Add new ones on a periodic basis.

What You'll Experience

Show Off Books on Facebook

Increase Online Donations

Circulate a Digital Flyer

Create an Electronic Press Kit

XVIII   Buzz a Book

Do you want to be the next John Irving or perhaps Washington Irving? There are over 150,000 books published each year. If you are a new author it is crucial to get the attention you need and Facebook is one of the best places to do it. At your fingertips is a potential audience of over 30 million registered users! To sell books you must be popular and Facebook is a great way to get fans and get noticed. In the following pages we'll show you how to explode your popularity on Facebook with over 55 tips and tricks to buzz your book.

1. Use the Correct Name

Having a name that is easy to remember on Facebook is important for your popularity and success. Sign up quickly to register your full name, which you use on your books, before an unofficial fan club or group takes it. If your name is already taken, get it as close to the name you promote as possible. For instance, if Pat Jones is the name you use as an author, register Patrick Jones on Facebook if Pat Jones is already taken. You get the picture. If you are promoting your stories in the public, now is not the time to be shy.

You have the option to use only the first letter of your last name on Facebook for privacy reasons, but this does not apply to authors in most cases. Use your full first and last names.

2. Register Your Books

If you are fortunate enough to have your own book published, Facebook lets you show it off on your profile . . . well at least the cover, which you can insert as your profile photo.

REMEMBER ISBN

ISBN stands for International Standard Book Number. Each book has one. Include it on your profile as this will allow Facebookers to find the book on Websites such as Amazon.com.

3. Theme Your Author Profile Photo

Your author profile photo should reflect the theme of your latest story or book. Readers want to believe in their authors and the best stories are often those experienced by the author in some fashion, even with fiction writing. Some of the best tales by J.D. Salinger and Earnest Hemingway are stories about being a solider that they both experienced in real life. If you have a partying photo on your profile, add a more serious one for your author profile to let everyone know you are a serious artist.

THIS INCLUDES ACTIVITIES & INTERESTS

The Activities and Interest areas of your profile are a great place to further build the theme of your book and the activities you've been participating in to research your next book or story. You have unlimited words to use for this purpose.

4. Add Facebook URL to Email Messages

Your Facebook URL can easily be added to outgoing email messages in the form of a hyperlink that your non-Facebook friends can click on to be taken to your profile. If Facebook is your only Web presence, it's important to build up friends and fans on your profile. Below is an example with everything from the http to just before the first > being the Facebook profile URL.

```
Put a link to your Facebook profile on AIM:
<a href=http://www.facebook.com/p/Andy_B/527300036>Facebook me!</a>
```

Visit the URL chapter of *Facebook Fanatic* to learn how to add this link into the messages of the Web's most popular email engines.

5. Focus on Favorite Quotes

The Favorite Quotes area of your interest section is important for authors. Here is where you show what authors, politicians, or religious figures inspire you. Fans like to see what makes their author's tick. So pay adequate attention to this area. Shakespeare is popular here. Of course, you can even quote yourself or a character from one of your stories! Two of the best (and free) quotes sites on the Internet are wisdomquotes.com and quoteland.com.

6. Get Friends and More Friends

Facebook popularity, just like real life, is centered on how many friends you have. To get a ton of fans—we're talking hundreds—you cannot just sit back and wait for them to beat a path to your Facebook digital door. Remember this magic Facebook formula:

> **Friends = Fans => Even More Fans**

People become your friend on Facebook because they like your stories or poems. When they have made this fan-status leap of faith, they will work to get you even more fans. That is the beauty of Facebook when trying to quickly build your fan base. People love to discover a great writer on Facebook. But this does not come overnight. Accept all friend requests and get this pile growing. As it does, so will your popularity.

7. Beat the Digital Pavement

There is an old proverb that says they who want friends must make themselves friendly, or something like that. The same applies to Facebook. Stop hiding within the confines of your profile and get out there and try to *make* new friends.

8. List Your Favorite Books

The last area of your interest section that is important to authors is the Favorite Books area. Here is where you let readers know what books impressed you and made you the writer you are today. Provide URL links to your favorite books (include your own) on

Amazon.com. To do this, visit the book on Amazon then copy and paste the URL in your browser window into the Favorite Books section. Tell fans to do the same, just the opposite, by copying and pasting it into their browser window to visit the page and buy the book.

9. Sell Photos and Bookcover Items

Viral marketing is spreading on Facebook. A great way to get in on the game is to sell photo items from QOOP. Never heard of it? Well, Facebook has teamed up with QOOP (QOOP.com), one of the Web's leading photo printing services. With QOOP you can order photos, posters, etc. You name it and QOOP can usually print your photos on it. You can even order books of photos. This is a great way to publish that photo book you've wanted to put out there or a novella with photos and text. Get creative and sell photos of yourself in many different ways on your Website, eBay or Facebook Marketplace.

10. Stock the Books Section

Facebook lets you add a Book Section to your profile and when you do, you can search for books and place their covers on the profile for the world of Facebookers to see. If you have published your own book, add it immediately to generate traffic. If you have not published yet, add books that you would recommend or that are similar in writing style so you can start getting friends who may like your book in the future.

FREE ADVERTISING IN THE NEW ADDITIONS COLUMN
When you add a new book it is displayed across Facebook in the New Additions column (across all networks) so you get free advertising for a brief period of time.

11. Leave a Comment with URL

When you add a new book to your profile, you can rate it and also post a comment. If it is your own book this is a great way to give some background. You have unlimited space in which to do this. Also include the URL to your Website or where Facebookers can purchase the book on site like Amazon.com and BN.com.

12. Let Your Feelings Be Known

Did Mom ever tell you to keep comments to yourself? Well, Facebook is not the place to follow Mom's instructions . . . if you want to become popular. Once you become friends with a well-trafficked profile or popular friend, send a comment over to keep your photo in the front and center. This includes other authors, books, films, Notes, and groups.

You have to get out there and cast your photo/comments net in as many popular places as possible to catch the most friends. If you are casting your net in shallow waters by making a few friend requests a day, you're not going to catch big fish. A great way to catch that digital mackerel is to become friends with featured profiles such as Facebook Diaries.

> If you get a new fan/friend, be sure to post a "Thanks for the Add" comment on The Wall to get even more exposure.

13. Leave a Great Comment About a Great Book

What if you could comment on the world's greatest books and let new fans discover you by clicking over to your profile? Well, you actually can. Add a book to your profile that is similar to your own and leave a thorough comment. Readers are then likely to click over to your profile and find your writings and learn all about you.

14. List Your Bio

Have writing experience? Did you win first prize in a short story competition for a magazine or school newspaper? You have unlimited characters to use in the About section of your profile. Do not be shy. This is a great place to give your bio as an author.

LIST THE BOOK SYNOPSIS

Another way to generate interest in your book is to provide its synopsis on your profile and/or the table of contents if it is a non-fiction title. Since you have unlimited words to use in interest sections, make the synopsis as long as you want.

15. Post First Chapter or Prologue

On your profile you have unlimited words to use in your interest sections. Here is where you should post a chapter or the prologue of your book. You can even post a short story! Get readers hooked so they will go out and buy your stuff. You should also place the URL at the end of the section where readers can purchase your book or view your regular Website.

16. List Book Signings

To get fans out to see you when signing books on the road, be sure to tell the time, date and place right on your profile. A great area for it is by posting a Note.

17. Get Good Reviews

Reviews are very important for a book and so are the comments. A person does not have to be a direct friend of the author to write one. Be sure to ask friends to read and review your books to create buzz on Facebook. Each reviewer can leave comments and rate the book from 1 to 5 stars.

AUTHOR REVIEWS

Yes, you can review your own book, but this is not going to be looked favorably upon by Facebook readers. Instead, try to get other Facebook authors to review your book.

18. Make a Few Polls

Polls are a good way to focus the attention of Facebook readers on a particular topic for your book. The best polls have one question and contain between 2 and 5 possible answers. Notes is a great place to conduct a poll or by leaving the question in a comment on The Wall.

AUTHOR POLL

Do a poll about yourself. This is a good way to generate fan base interaction and to gage what readers would like to see from you in the future. You can even poll about the ending of your stories to see what fans would have liked differently.

Here are some other poll ideas. Most are general in nature, but will make your profile sticky.

Great Poll Ideas Table 18.A
➢ Trivia about your favorite short story, book, etc.
➢ Best quote from favorite novel?
➢ Best first sentence from favorite novel?
➢ What do you fear the most?
➢ Questions about the best city or place to go on vacation
➢ Which amusement park has the best rollercoasters?
➢ Best poem in each genre
➢ Who will win a sporting event or election?
➢ Best book of the last 100 years (Hint: *Catcher in the Rye*)

19. Show Your Cover Image

If your book is not widely available so that it can be searched within Facebook, scan in a cover of your book and get it on your profile. Instead of showing your face as the default profile picture, show your book's cover. This is a great way to make your photo stand apart from the thousands of faces on Facebook.

20. Be a Note Hog

Notes are vital to making your profile "sticky" and for ensuring your writing stays in the minds of readers when lots of other authors are trying to muscle you out. If you are doing book events on the road, get a laptop with wireless Internet access so you can stay in touch with fans. Post a Note every day or multiple times a day, letting them know when and where you will be doing the next event. You are a writer after all! Notes should be second nature. They love to read about experiences on the road! Create a URL hyperlink at the end of your Note.

> On your profile conduct an interview in question-and-answer fashion. Do it in Notes and watch your fan base grow.

21. Post a Contest

A great way to get fans reading your Notes is to have periodic contests. How do you have one? Easy. State on your profile that you will be having a Note contest in the next few weeks. On the day you decide, post a trivia question about your book or one of your book characters, etc on your Note. The first one to answer correctly by leaving a comment gets an autographed book. While you can edit a Note comment and the new post date will be the edit date, you cannot backdate a Note comment on Facebook so you can tell who is truly the first to answer.

22. Get a Publicity Manager

Having a professional outfit behind you for promotions is key to success on Facebook. It is best if your publicity manager is already on Facebook and they know the site backwards and forwards. You need someone who can tout your growing popularity to Facebook advertisers and work marketing deals for you. Search Facebook for "publicity manager" or "publicist" and give them a poke or send a message.

23. Post a Video Reading

The coolest thing in books has nothing to do with paper or ink. It is actually a way authors can do selected readings from their books or an entire short story. Video readings are all the rage. Do one and post it on Facebook or YouTube. Some of the coolest videos are homemade ones with a documentary feel. Many are shot in black and white of the author. You certainly do not need an expensive video camera for this. Visit the video section of *Facebook Fanatic* to learn how to get a video from your camera or hard drive onto Facebook.

What is key to getting your shorts on mobile devices such as a cellphone or video iPod is to convert your video files into the correct format. Cellphones play video in 3GP format. For PCs Xilisoft has published its 3GP Converter at xilisoft.com for downloading. Keep the file size as small as possible to limit the download time on mobile devices.

> At ffmpegx.com you can download free cellphone conversion software for the Mac.

For video iPods there is a special iPod format. You can download MoviePod at nullriver.com in formats that work for the PC or Mac. The file can be of any size. Apple requires all films and shorts to be sized in a 640x480 format to play on video iPods.

24. Post Book Related Videos

If at the moment you do not have a video of you reciting a story, post a video that is book related on your profile about another writer. There are some great ones about Edgar Allan Poe and quotations from *The Raven*.

POST A VIDEO FROM OTHER SITES

Is there a sweet video on YouTube that shows how books are made? If you don't have a video of you being interviewed or doing a reading, show one of these videos by placing it in your HTML Box.

25. Attach Video to Email Messages

It sounds complicated, but it is easy to attach your video interviews to email messages. After the video is uploaded click the Share link next to it. Alternatively, you can always just copy the video URL and email or IM that link to your fans. Since it is a hyperlink, all they have to do is click on the link to be taken to the Facebook profile where the video is showing.

26. Display Up to 10 Books

Click on Edit next to any book you are showing in your profile and you will be taken to the book settings page. There you have the option of showing up to ten books at once with the default being two. Add books, especially if they're yours.

27. Circulate Your Cover

We've all seen how magazines and national newspapers get plastered with the latest fiction offerings by big name authors. Now, even if you are a new author, you can do the same thing, but digitally, and reach the entire world. All it takes is for you to post an image ("digital flyer") on your profile along with the HTML code for showing the flyer. If you have a .jpg file of your book cover, you have a flyer created already. Have fans distribute it for you. Then fans can just copy and paste the code onto their Website to show your flyer. The can also copy and paste the code into their Notes and HTML Box on Facebook!

Circulate a Digital Flyer Table 18.B
➤ Create the flyer using a graphic program such as Microsoft Paint and save in JPEG (.jpg) format ➤ Upload cover image to Facebook ➤ Use this HTML tag to show flyer on your profile: <a href="http://www.Facebook.com/AUTHORURL" target="_blank"><img src="FACEBOOKURLOFCOVERIMAGE" width="319" height="413"></a> ➤ Display HTML under flyer and tell fans to paste it onto their Website

28. Conduct a Video Interview

Fans love to hear how books came into being. Sit on your favorite sofa or in front of a bookcase and record a video interview. Last, upload the video to Facebook or YouTube and show it on your profile.

<u>A LITTLE PLANNING IS GOOD</u>
Get questions laid out beforehand and think of what you are going to say so the video does not have to be cropped. Rehearse or you will sound canned and boring.

29. Create "Share on Facebook" HTML

Facebook provides you a basic Share on Facebook HTML link to put on your Website. This makes it easy for visitors to click it and share the content on Facebook with their friends. Fine. But if you really want to make HTML links come alive, there are special HTML meta tags that you must insert to preview the content. See the Posted Items chapter of *Facebook Fanatic* for linking options. The minor problem with sharing content using these links, however, is that they only provide a link and little else. There are no meta tags that tell Facebook what type of content it is (audio, video, image, text, etc.). Add the following basic tags to ensure the title of your story and a short description are imported into Facebook. This also includes the initial image of your content, if it is an image or video, which is displayed on Facebook

Meta Tags

<meta name="title" content="'Google Advertising Guerrilla Tactics' book published by BottleTree" />
<meta name="description" content="Learn the tips and tricks you need to make money on AdWords." />
<link rel="image_src" href="http://www.bottletreebooks.com/GuerrillaTactics.jpg" />

> The title and summary tags are the minimum requirements for any preview, so make sure to include these two.

Basic Content Tags

An example short story could have the following:
<meta name="title" content="The Legend of Sleepy Hollow" />
<meta name="description" content="Icabod Crain and the Headless Horseman. Need we say more?" />
<link rel="image_src" href="URLofCOVERIMAGE.jpg" />
As shown, title contains the preview title, description contains the preview summary and image_src contains the preview image.

Type of Content Tag

You may specify the type of content being shared by using the following tag:
<meta name="medium" content="medium_type" />
Valid values for *medium_type* are "audio", "image", "video", "news", "Note" and "mult".

*To make videos embeddable on Facebook, please send a request to developers-help@facebook.com. This request should include the domain names of the values you will use for the video source URL (in the video_src link tag above). You must do this to ensure your videos play correctly.

30. Link to "Search Inside the Book" on Amazon

If potential new readers can browse through pages of your book on Amazon.com or Google Book, be sure to provide a link on your profile since Facebook does not show the inside of books, only covers.

31. Compile an Electronic Press Kit

Without leaving their wingback leather chairs with inlaid studs, publishers and agents can check you out. That is the beauty of Facebook. You no longer have to physically print a press kit filled with pictures, writing samples, and descriptions when you can have a much better (and less expensive one) on your profile. Now all you need is a great profile with an electronic press kit and, of course, great stories. Key items to include in your digital press kit are shown below.

Key Items for a Digital Press Kit on Facebook Table 18.C
➢ Biography/Experience ➢ Education ➢ Interviews ➢ Photos ➢ Awards ➢ Publications or writing samples

32. Get Signed With an Agent

Getting signed with an agent is easier said than done. There are simply no A-B-C steps to follow. Never fear. Facebook offers a number of tools to get you discovered. Your profile is your calling card to getting popular and recognized on Facebook. If it is unprofessional, no agents will come calling. There is simply too much competition. Once you have a great profile with a digital press kit, search for book agents on the Web and email them a hyperlink so they can click over to your profile. Visit the hyperlink section of *Facebook Fanatic* to learn how to automatically attach your link to messages on major email sites.

CHECK OUT AUTHORS IN YOUR GENRE

If you find an author on Facebook that writes in a similar genre and they have already signed with an agent, find out which one from their profile or look in the credits section of their book. Then, approach a competitive agent and market why your book is better. This is guerrilla book marketing at its finest.

33. Podcast a Serial Novel

In 1996 Stephen King published a popular serial novel called "The Green Mile". It was published in 6 paperback installments. Use this same concept to publish a serial story on Notes or in an interest section. Each allow for unlimited words.

34. Get Fans to Contact iTunes

If you have created an audio book or Podcast, but it is not downloadable from iTunes, get Facebook fans to email Apple. Eventually Apple will get the hint that there is a market for your audio books on iTunes.

35. Post iTunes Link Maker on Facebook Profile

What is iTunes Link Maker? It is a dedicated Apple connection that lets you link directly to your audio book (or Podcast for that matter) on iTunes so fans can pay to download it.

Once you get an audio book on iTunes link to it from your Facebook profile. Follow this link to get iTunes Link Maker today and remember that you will have to incorporate the link on your Facebook profile so that fans can copy and paste it into their browser: http://phobos.apple.com/WebObjects/MZSearch.woa/wa/itmsLinkMaker.

36. Use iTunes Producer

iTunes Producer is a free Apple utility that allows you to convert audio books from almost any digital format to ACC, Apple's dedicated digital recording format.

You will need to have files converted to ACC in order for them to be downloadable on iTunes. So, after Facebook fans clamor for your audio books to be included on iTunes, convert them to ACC and you will be all set to launch. To get iTunes Producer you first must sign up for iTunes Label Connect: http://www.apple.com/itunes/musicmarketing/ and then follow the instructions to download.

37. Show Off Fans

The number of fans you have as an author is very important. They are the number of friends you have. Tons of fans along with great stories can get you signed with an agent. So stock up on friends before contacting an agent on Facebook.

38. Link Your Way to Success

Linking is the best way to get fans from your Facebook profile over to your Website. One click and they are there. While you are at it, ensure you hyperlink back from your Website to your Facebook profile. You can find a bunch of free linking icons that are provided by Facebook as Facebook Badges and with them you can provide a splashy graphic that lets the world click over to your Facebook profile. You have total control on what info you place in them. Got your own personal Website apart from Facebook? If so, this is a great place for your badge.

Steps to Get a Facebook Badge Table 18.D
➢ Login to Facebook ➢ Click on Profile ➢ Select create a profile badge under your photo

39. Have a Facebook Filmmaker Use Your Story

There are tons of new and independent filmmakers on Facebook trying to break into the business just as you are trying to do with your book. Contact a few and see if they would like a royalty free license to use your story in an upcoming short film. If you have a screenplay, all the better. It's not as hard as it sounds to find a filmmaker on Facebook.

40. Start a Group About Your Books

Groups within the school and college section of Facebook are a fantastic way to get noticed. If you attended a school that has a book group, this is a good place to get known. Also, if you were in a fraternity/sorority, this is a good way to get your name out. You should also ask fans to start a group if they desire. If a fan club about you is started, post in it regularly! The fans will love it. You should also post in groups that discuss the theme of one of your books or stories. Even if you do have a group dedicated to you as an author, it is always good to post in a book-related group.

41. Start a Thread in a Group

Practice your knitting because a good way to get noticed on Facebook is to start interesting threads under book groups. And when you do, your photo and link to your profile will be shown. This is a good way to get more clicks to your profile.

42. Locate Book Groups and Get Active

How do you find all these great book groups on Facebook? Search Facebook for "books" and you will find 500+ groups related to books. Some focus on particular genres, others on one author like J.D. Salinger and still others on just one book. You can also search on "Authors" to find 500+ more groups. Find one related to you, join it, and get active.

43. List Groups Where You Belong

There are tons of cool groups out there. If you belong to some of them, why not list them on your profile by ensuring the list group privacy setting is disabled? Ensure these groups relate to books or writing in general and you will not turn off fans.

44. Protect Persona From Posers

In developing your identity as an author, it is just as important to guard against Facebook imposters. People pretending to be authors can occur on Facebook. State at the top of your profile that this is your "official" Facebook profile.

45. Post Items for Sale on eBay

A lot of new authors offer signed books for sale on eBay.com to help out sales. If you are doing this, you can show these items on your profile too, so fans can follow the link to buy your books. Do not forget autographed books and T-shirts, which are always hot sellers. Here are the steps.

Hyperlink to eBay Table 18.E
➢ Post item for sale on eBay ➢ Visit page on eBay where item is for sale ➢ Click in the browser URL window and copy the URL link ➢ Paste the URL into an interest section or Notes

46. Post Items for Sale on Google Base

Google Base (www.base.google.com) has been cutting into eBay's business. One of the main reasons is because it does not charge for listing or selling items. Google makes its money off click advertising. In addition, listing items on Google Base gets them automatically included in Google's search results.

Hyperlink to Google Base Table 18.F
➢ Post item for sale on Google Base ➢ Visit page on Google Base where item is for sale ➢ Click in the browser URL window and copy the URL link ➢ Paste the link into any interest section of your profile

47. Free Novellas and Shorts

When you are struggling to make it as an author, it seems counterintuitive to give away your stories. But this is one of the best ways to get new fans. Let Facebook users read your free short stories or novellas and watch your popularity soar. Be sure to type the story first in a word processor so you can do a spell check. Then copy and paste the story into the Read It section of your author profile.

48. Share Favorite Books

Want to easily let readers know about your books and those that inspired you? Get the Books application and you are quickly on your way to unlocking your bookshelf.

Search Facebook for "Books app" and get this application to impress fans. Writers are readers first!

49. Upload New stories Continuously

It's all about the stories for most of your fans. To keep your profile sticky, upload new short stories every month if possible. Since your interest sections have unlimited words available, you can put a complete short story within it. So get writing and uploading to keep fans coming back for more.

KEEP YOUR SHORTS SHORT

Long short stories are hard to read on a Facebook profile, so try to keep your short stories . . . short if you are going to display the entire text on your profile.

50. Enable the Amazon.com Honor System

What is the Amazon.com Honor System? It is a program where fans can give you money right on your Website by clicking on the link. Fans can give you as little as $1 USD at a time. This is a good way to fund your Website and to get money for all those free stories you are posting. To sign up follow this link: http://zme.amazon.com/exec/varzea/fx-register/login.

Be sure to link to your Amazon.com Honor System page on your Facebook profile and let profile visitors know that they can give money in support of your writing.

51. Pick a Prominent Friend Position

Facebook popularity is centered around how many friends you have and not only the number of friends, which is very important, but also the quality of friends. What do we mean by the *quality* of friends? It is very simple. In the Facebook world the quality of friends is directly linked to their celebrity bling. Having movie stars, sports stars, and top name bands on your friend list will launch your popularity. For better or worse, people are judged by the status level of their friends.

FRIEND ORDER CAN BE CHANGED

The order of your friends is not set in stone. You can move friends to the top of your list at any time. This can work for you and against you. Ask fans to move you to the top of their friends' list on their profiles for better exposure.

52. Create Book Club Questions

Another good way to buzz a book on Facebook is to include a list of questions for book groups so that they can discuss your book. Create a new Note entry on your profile and list out a bunch of questions for a book discussion group. Then you can list the answers to these questions at a later time and see if they agree with those discussed by the group.

53. Publish Free Articles to Increase Profile Traffic

Post free articles about your short stories or books in general to generate free clicks over to your profile. That's right, there are a number of fine Websites that accept articles on writing or most any general topic. Blogs and other sites may publish them on the Web for free and link back to your profile. Here is a list of some of the best ones: ContentDesk.com, Ezine Articles.com, GoArticles.com, and IdeaMarketers.com.

54. Show Fans the Future

Fans want to know what you will be reading in the future to get an idea of where you might be heading as an artist. With the iRead application you can see the books of your fans and list those you want to read in the future.

This is an excellent way to see what things your fans read to get an idea of the direction where your next story should head.

55. List a Great Quiz

Publish a quiz about yourself or your books. Let's say you don't want to publish a quiz about yourself or your books, you just want to keep things interesting on your profile. The options for alternate quizzes are only limited by your imagination. Name your quiz whatever you would like and start creating it. In table 18.G are some rad ideas to get you started.

Great Quiz Ideas Table 18.G
➢ Trivia about your favorite band, movie, TV show, sports team, book, etc.
➢ Questions about your school are cool.
➢ Any quiz about the theme of your profile (fast cars, basketball, Goth, etc.).
➢ Random quiz with questions about all kinds of different topics to see how smart your visitors are.
➢ Good in math? Create a math quiz.
➢ Make an anagram quiz by arranging letters of, for example, the name of popular authors (e.g., HONKS A JET = John Keats; A SHEEP'S RAKE = Shakespeare). Four potential answers are given and the right one must be guessed.
➢ Ask trivia about your friends and the results will be reported to you via email. This is a great way to find out intimate details about your friends!

SEARCH THE NET

A search of the Internet for "Quiz Ideas" or "Quiz Questions" will yield some great quiz Websites that will help you build cool quizzes about all things in the book world.

56. Link to Stories on TaleSale.com

TaleSale.com is a great Website that lets anyone sell short stories in PDF format or audio short stories in MP3 format. Launching in late 2007, TaleSale creates a community of readers and writers that share similar tastes in short stories.

Gone are the days where you have to wait up to six months to learn if your short story will be published by a magazine. Now you can sell your short stories and make money off each sale almost immediately! Link to your TaleSale profile from your Facebook Notes and direct readers to buy your PDF and MP3 stories on TaleSale.com.

What You'll Experience

What to Do If You Break Up with Someone

How Teachers Can Remove False Profiles

Make Money Off Your Profile

Search Facebook from Any Search Engine

XIX   More Tips & Tricks

1. Search Facebook from Search Engines

You must have a public profile on Facebook for it to be searchable on Internet search engines. Even if you do, the searcher must have a Facebook account to view the public profile. Anyone with a Facebook account can the Internet's search engines to look for people on Facebook. Simply type the word "Facebook" in the search box followed by your search name and the words "public profile". This is because the title of every public Facebook profile page looks like this: FACEBOOK | FIRST NAME LAST NAME (OR INITIAL)'S PUBLIC PROFILE.

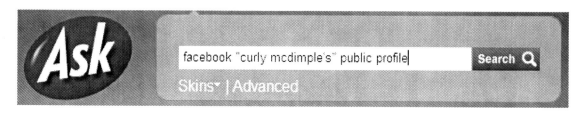

Note the 's at the end of the name. Ask.com works great by searching on the title. At the present, Google will not find any pages using this exact title search method as it does *not* recognize the 's. Be sure to include the word Facebook a few times in your About section and Notes for your profile to rank higher in the search engines when a person searches on your name from the outside.

2. Look Into the Mirror
Here is a nice little Facebook hack that will reveal mirror indexes on Facebook:

Type it into Google and watch what happens! You can perform this hack on any Website just for kicks.

3. Detect Spam Contact Messages
Spam is not as prevalent on Facebook as on most Internet email sites, but it does exist. People use software programs to generate thousands of automatic friend requests. No one wants to spend time on spam that fools you into thinking it is a genuine friend request. Visit the requester's profile and see if they are legit. Many spammers build a very basic profile and then launch the program to thousands of people. If you find a spammer, immediately add them to your blocked list.

4. Facebook Help Button
Need assistance with something on Facebook? Remember the Facebook help link located at the very bottom of the screen.

Clicking it will bring you to Facebook's latest help guide on all things Facebook. If your questions are still not answered, you can always email Facebook.

5. What to Do If You Break Up With Someone
If you break up with someone on Facebook (especially if you are the dumper instead of the dumpee) you may be in for a lashing on your profile. But there are a couple of ways to prevent unwanted comments and steps to take as soon as you break up.

First, delete the ex from your friend list. They will not be notified and you will automatically be erased from their friend list along with your contact information. Since they will now be off your friend list, they cannot comment on your profile page and the whole Facebook community will not see what negative things they have to say.

Second, you must block your ex.

Steps to Block a Person on Facebook Table 19.A
➢ Login to your profile ➢ Select Privacy in upper right-hand corner ➢ Under Block People, input the person's name or search for them and add them to your block list

You do not want a jilted significant ex posting vindictive comments on The Wall. You can always delete any comments your ex posts on The Wall or any comments for that matter!

Third, Let's say your ex-boyfriend is on Facebook and even though you have broken up, you remain friends. It is reasonable to perhaps not give your ex full access to your profile. On Facebook this is easy. You can limit profile access to anyone and here is how to do it.

Steps to Limit Profile Access on Facebook Table 19.B
➢ Login to your profile ➢ Select Privacy in upper right-hand corner ➢ Under limited Profile, input person's name or search for them and add them ➢ Select the portions of your profile that will be limited access

6. Sorry Parents, You Are Out of Luck

Even parents of Facebook users cannot have access to their child's accounts. Facebook states that federal and most state laws forbid it from giving access to a person's account without their permission . . . even to a parent. This applies to school teachers who may also want to see a student's Facebook account that has been made private.

7. The Hover Mystery

At the bottom of each Facebook page is the typical copyright right notice: Facebook © 2008. Fine. But if you move your mouse pointer over the © you will see a two or three digit number pop up. There is much conjecture over what this **number** represents. It is likely the host server number or perhaps an alien code counting **down** the end of time. ☺

8. How to Delete Your Facebook Profile and Account

Are all those hours on Facebook making your life unproductive elsewhere? Are you tired of your profile? Here is how to delete your Account . . . permanently . . . get it gone! We are not kidding. This will trash your account, your profile, photos, Notes, videos addresses, content and maybe make you disappear as a human being. Click on Account in the upper right of the screen → Deactivate Account. Be sure to follow the directions to a T. Here are the reasons you must pick from to deactivate your account. We like the first one the best.

Reasons Why Deactivating Account Table 19.C
➤ Facebook is resulting in social drama for me
➤ I don't feel safe on the site
➤ I don't find Facebook useful
➤ I don't understand how to use the site
➤ I have another Facebook account
➤ I need to fix something in my account
➤ I receive too many emails from Facebook
➤ I spend too much time using Facebook
➤ Other
➤ This is temporary. I'll be back.

Once your account is deactivated, friends can still invite you to events, tag you in their photos, or invite you to join their groups. Simply opt out to stop receiving these email invites.

FIRST STEP TO BEING REINCARNATED ON FACEBOOK
Maybe your Facebook profile is unattractive to potential new employers or maybe you just want to delete your Account, lie low during finals, and resurface as a Facebook butterfly with a new Account and profile. The first step is to delete your Account and then sign up for a new one later. Think of it as a Facebook redo! You can reactivate your old account at anytime if you need to use it later.

Keep in mind that posts and comments elsewhere on Facebook will remain. So if you have posted bad things on a teacher's Wall, this will *not* be deleted when you account is deleted.

9. Start Over Without Deleting Your Account

There may come a time in your Facebook life that you want to start all over. Don't you wish you could do that in real life? Anyway, in your virtual life this is possible. Whether it is because you don't like your friends or you don't like the look of your profile or you want to appear to be a newbie on Facebook. Whatever the reason, do not take the drastic measure of deleting your account when you can make it appear brand new.

Wipe Facebook Profile Clean   **Table 19.D**
➢ Change your Facebook screen name   ➢ Change your email listed with Facebook   ➢ Change/delete your photos   ➢ Delete everything in your interest sections; keep the text if you want   ➢ Remove your friends' comments   ➢ Delete all postings to The Wall   ➢ Remove all Facebook applications you've added

10. Tile Friends

Facebook only displays six friends on your profile and you must click "view all" to see them in column format. There is a cool hack, however, to get around this so you can see all your friends' profile photos in tile format. It is only two steps.

Tile Friend Photos   **Table 19.E**
➢ Click on My Friends in the left-hand column of your profile   ➢ Select the --- dashed line that appears in the Show dropdown menu

11. Make Money Off Facebook Profile

If you have a Website that displays Internet ads such as Google's AdSense (adsense.google.com) or Yahoo's Publisher Network (publisher.yahoo.com), you can place a text link on your profile. Visitors will then be able to copy and paste it into their browser and be taken to your Website. This will drive even more traffic to your Website and potentially bring in more click revenue for you! Remember that since Facebook will not allow Javascript, you cannot show these ads directly on your profile even with the HTML Box application.

12. Teachers – Remove False Profiles

The days of drawing cartoons of teachers in math class is over. Now cyberhooligans (you know who you are) post false teacher profiles on Facebook. Some have the teacher's photo as a whale or a donkey with outlandish interests. Posting these profiles is against Facebook's Terms of Use. If you are a teacher and your false profile is on Facebook, you can get it removed by contacting Facebook directly at info@facebook.com or by clicking "report abuse" under the profile photo.

13. Scrub Profile Before a Job Search

If you are looking for a killer summer job or the position of a lifetime after graduating college, be sure to go over your profile with a fine toothcomb. Ensure that before you go on your job-hunt that you get any embarrassing photos or comments off your profile. Savvy employers are now searching Facebook to see what your personal life is all about. If it is nothing but partying, you may never get a job interview from certain employers.

SEARCH YOUR INTERVIEWER

You can potentially turn the tables on an interviewer for a new job by checking Facebook to see if *they* have a profile of their own. If so, it is a great way to view their personal interests before you get on the job interview.

14. Don't Lose Facebook Profile When You Leave School

Here is the problem: You are leaving college and will be losing your college email, which it so happens is the email you use as your login ID on Facebook. Relax. Facebook has it covered. Follow these steps.

Keep Facebook Profile After You Leave School Table 19.F
➢ First, get a new email address ➢ Update the email address with Facebook by going to the Account page ➢ Click on the Settings tab ➢ Update email and new address ➢ Click Save

If you get a new job when you get out of school, be sure to add a work network in addition to your school network to your Facebook account.

15. Launch a Paid-for-Poll

For as little as $6 Facebook lets you take a poll of almost any demographic on its network of 30 million users. Want to know who people are going to vote for in Olive Branch, Mississippi? Do guys were boxers, briefs or nothing in Leeds? This is a huge tool for advertisers and focus groups. Just click on Polls at the bottom of any Facebook page.

16. How to Unblock Facebook

Does the school system administrator have you down because they've blocked Facebook access? Has your college banned Facebook as a result of bandwidth and productivity concerns? Don't worry. Facebook hacks are here. A popular way to block Facebook is for a network administrator to add it as a restricted site on all computers. Here is how to unblock Facebook as a restricted site.

Unblock Facebook Table 19.G
➤ Select the Tools menu within Internet Explorer
➤ Pick Internet Options → Click on Security → Pick Restricted Sites
➤ Select and Remove Facebook.com → Apply the new settings

Alternatively, you can visit a proxy redirection site that tricks your network into believing you are on a normal Website when you have actually been redirected to Facebook. Visit proxy.org to obtain a list of over 4000 proxy sites! Or you can use the Web's language translation services, which will make the Web translation site act like a proxy server for Facebook. For example, on Google do an English-to-English translation of Facebook: google.com/translate?langpair=en|en&u=www.Facebook.com and you have created your own proxy server using Google!

17. Players Unite

We do not recommend this, but if you are a "player" or better yet "playa" on Facebook and want to have multiple boyfriends/girlfriends without any of the other knowing, you may be able to pull it off. But it will be a lot of work. The biggest stumbling block is your basic info that tells the world your relationship status. Under your limited profile privacy setting, block anyone on your list from seeing your basic info. Then add new boyfriends/girlfriends at will. Be careful of the events you attend as this might blow your cover!

18. Pimp Our Book!

Have you gotten new friends because of the tips in *Facebook Fanatic*? Has your popularity gone through the roof? Are you selling more songs, films or books from the buzz tips you've learned? If you want to make money off the hottest Facebook book on the market, this is how to do it.

Join **Associates**

Under the free Amazon.com Associates program you can sign up and get an icon for *Facebook Fanatic* to put on your Website. When a person buys the book by clicking on the icon, Amazon.com pays you up to 6% of the sales price. Sign up for the Amazon.com Associates program: http://associates.amazon.com/gp/associates/join/002-5352461-2272849 and start making money!

MySpace Maxed Out
Explode Your Popularity, Buzz Your Band, and Secure Your Privacy on MySpace

Become MySpace royalty. Explode your career. Secure your privacy. With over 150 million users MySpace is the world's largest social networking site. Feel lost and overwhelmed? Don't be! "MySpace Maxed Out" is an extensive guide on all areas of MySpace. Dominate it instead of being just part of it. Got a band? Learn 75 ways to get thousands of fans. Are you a filmmaker, politician or author? Find out how to launch your career to 150 million potential customers. Learn how to get insanely popular. Concerned about privacy? Read how to secure it in every area. Here are a few of the topics covered: 75 Ways to Buzz Your Band; Popularity Tips and Tricks to Make You Internet Royalty; HTML & CCS Boot Camp with Tons of Code; Coolest Profile Names and URLs; Get Celebrities and Famous Bands as Your Friend; MySpaceIM A to Z; Podcast Your Way to Stardom on MySpace; Be a Note Hog; Go Underground on MySpace with Little Used Privacy Settings; Make Money Off Your Videos; Authors: Over 55 Ways to Buzz Your Book; and Filmmakers: Over 70 Ways to Get Films Recognized. Politicians: Over 40 ways to zoom your political campaign. Rule MySpace!

Book $16.31 USD
bottletreebooks.com/myspace.htm

Google Advertising Guerrilla Tactics
Google Advertising A-Z Plus 150 Killer AdWords Tips & Tricks

"Google Advertising Guerrilla Tactics" is an extensive guide on all aspects of Google advertising and provides over 150 killer tips and tricks for getting the most clicks at the lowest cost. Stop wasting AdWords money and learn the guerrilla tactics you need to beat your competition. Here are but a few of the topics covered: How to Get Free AdWords Coupons - Breaking Down the Quality Score to Get More Clicks and Higher Ranking at Less Cost-Per-Click - Bid Traps: How to Prevent and Exploit Them - Vital Ad Stylization Techniques - Where to Find Keywords Your Competitors Will Not Think to Look - Ways to Use Abbreviations, Plurals and Misspellings - Most Popular Search Terms for Over 15 Holidays - Best Image Ad Sizes - Image Ad Colors that Will Wreck Your Campaign - Site Target Your Way to Quick Success - Search and Content Network Bid Strategies - How to Use Froogle, Google Base, Google Book Search, Google Catalogs, and Zeitgeist to Get Free Sales Conversions - The Key to Getting #1 Placement on Google - Industry Examples of Crucial Advertising Do's and Don'ts. If you want to beat your competition by getting more AdWords clicks at the lowest cost then "Google Advertising Guerrilla Tactics" is a must.

Book $24.48 USD
bottletreebooks.com/GuerrillaTactics.htm

Entire Tales & Poems of Edgar Allan Poe
Photographic & Annotated Edition

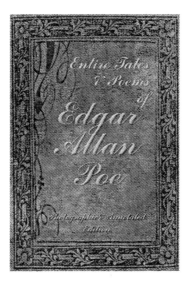

. . . if you were going to get a collected works of Poe, I'd recommend this above all others. –Joanna Daneman, Amazon.com Top Ten Reviewer

This book contains a foreword by **Andrew Barger,** along with his annotations, word definitions, foreign language translations, and background information about Poe's stories and poems that provide insight into their underlying meaning. Photographs of Poe's many loves and the poems they sent to him are included. The poems are set forth to display the exchange of poetry from and to Poe as it unfolded. Also included are five little-known Poe tales: "[The Bloodhounds]," "[The Rats of Park Theatre]," and "Some Secrets of the Magazine Prison House." Here is a sampling of tales and poems included: "Annabel Lee," "The Bells," "The Black Cat," "The Cask of Amontillado," "The Conqueror Worm," "A Descent into the Maelstrom," "The Fall of the House of Usher," "The Gold-Bug," "The Haunted Palace," "The Masque of the Red Death," "MS. Found in a Bottle," "Murders in the Rue Morgue," "The Pit and the Pendulum," "The Premature Burial," "The Purloined Letter," "The Raven," "Some Words with a Mummy," "The System of Doctor Tarr and Professor Fether," "The Tell-Tale Heart," and "Ulalume." Photographically experience the poems and stories of the author who invented the mystery genre and defined the horror genre.

Hardback $35.49 | Paperback $25.06 USD
bottletreebooks.com/EntireTales.htm

AdSense Unleashed
AdSense A-Z Plus 175 Killer Tips and Tricks

"AdSense Unleashed" shows you how to generate money quickly and easily as an AdSense publisher. The book provides 175 killer tips for attracting clicks on ads shown on your Website. Learn which ad units get the most clicks and where to put them on your Website or Note. Also included is a huge list of the highest paying keywords in the United States, United Kingdom, Australia, Canada, and Ireland. Here are a few of the topics covered:

How to Get Free Content on the Web - Best Ad Sizes and Where to Place Them in Articles, Notes and on Regular Websites - The AdWords-AdSense Revenue Loop – How to Block Site-Targeted Ads - Review of the Google AdSense Patents and Pending Patent Application - AdSense for Search Box Placement Strategies - How to Blend All the Various Ad Colors with Your Website - AdSense Referral Strategies - Alternate Ads and How to Use Them - How Expanded Text Ads Get You More Revenue - Site-Flavored AdSense for Search - Use Filters to Keep Competitor Ads Off Your Site - Ad Units and Framed Websites - Link Unit Strategies - How themed Ad Units Get More Clicks - Animated Ads and How to Block Them. If you want to unlock the revenue potential of your Website today, "AdSense Unleashed" is a must.

Printed in the United States
122003LV00004B/1-12/A